MW01518769

Rootless

Nigel Scotchmer

Excudebat Nigellus Scotchmer Archicommentator ironicus
cavillosusque

Front cover and frontispiece by Hara Papatheodorou

Back cover image by Marion Voysey

Global ISBN: (Hardcover) 978-1-962224-43-7

(Softcover) 978-1-962224-42-0

(eBook) 978-1-962108-52-2

AMAZON BOOK PUBLISHING CENTRAL

Library and Archives Canada Cataloguing in Publication

Title: Rootless/ Nigel S. Scotchmer

Name: Scotchmer, Nigel Stephen, 1956 – author

Identifier: Canadiana (Hardback) ISBN 978-1-7380953-1-5

Canadiana (eBook) ISBN 978-1-7380953-2-2

Canadiana (Softcover) ISBN 978-1-7380953-0-8

For Taliska, Adur, and little Emily

"And must not we swim and try and reach the shore, while

hoping that Arion's Dolphin or some other miraculous help

may save us?"

Plato, *The Republic, Bk. V, 453 e*

Contents

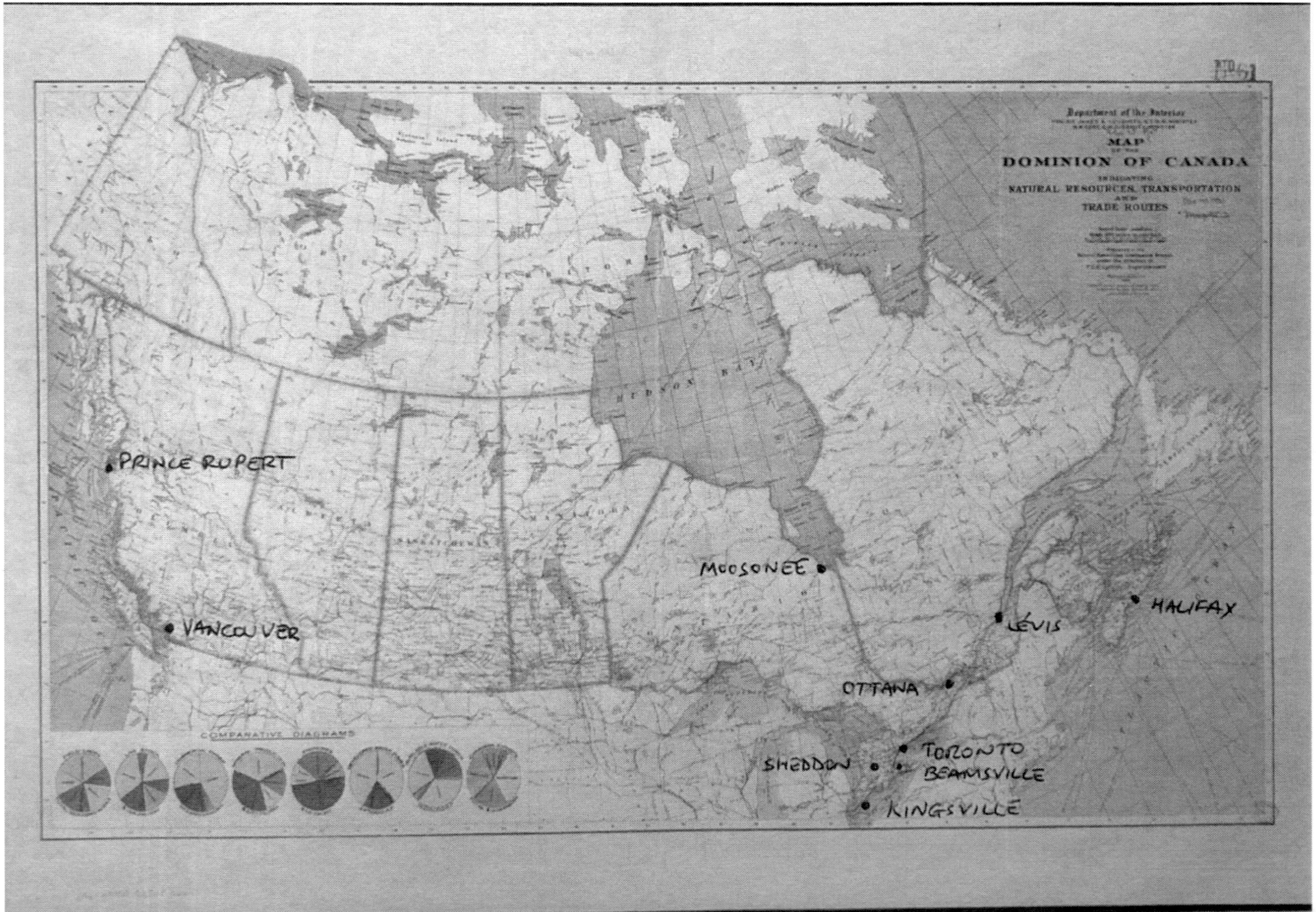
Department of the Interior
MAP
OF THE
DOMINION OF CANADA
INDICATING
NATURAL RESOURCES, TRANSPORTATION
AND
TRADE ROUTES
HUDSON BAY
PRINCE RUPERT
VANCOUVER
MOOSONEE
LÉVIS
HALIFAX
OTTAWA
TORONTO
BEAMSVILLE
SHEDDON
KINGSVILLE
COMPARATIVE DIAGRAMS

Part I

Liassez-moi Danser

(Let Me Dance!)

Pour toujours et à jamais, for ever and ever, Françoise Dorléac dances for me. As her career was reaching to the stars, she drove too fast in her Renault 10, which rolled and burned, killing her in excruciating pain. I vouch that life imitates art; Oscar Wilde was correct.

Freedom, 1976

"Shit! It's gone!"

I flew back from my revelry on the plains, where everything is wild and free, and looked at my Venezuelan cowboy, who was aghast.

"It's gone! It's gone!"

Worried, I looked down at his shrinking penis to see that; indeed, the condom was gone.

No more the blue sky, the sun, the open llanos, and the long grasses, galloping on horses with Carbonel, with the wind in my hair, over low hills; with the Andes behind us in the distance, our souls together. "I love, I cry, I sing, I dream" – no more. Down to earth, I came, like ordure under foot, crushed and mixed with the grass and its putrefying smell in the heat.

The Men's Residence at Victoria College had a bell tower, built over a gate, which was also one of the residences called, imaginatively, Gate House. I had noticed there was a doorway to the bell tower next to the gate and thought it would be fun to climb the tower. This door, half hidden by an overgrown bush, had a cruciform lock on the door. These cruciform locks looked as though the key would be some type of oversized Philips screwdriver. I had read about these famous Zeiss Ikon locks in a book of World War II prisoners of war locked up in Colditz Castle. They had been difficult to pick. I had pointed it out to Carbonel. History and intrigue –

reading about escaping from a POW camp and now climbing a forbidden tower with a vintage lock suddenly made history come alive all the more!

"'Es el mismo m'sieu con otro cachimbo' – it is the same guy with yet another gimmick," said Carbonel, looking dismissively at the lock.

"I bet you can't pick that lock." I knew his response.

"Watch me."

This was to be the start of my first fling, and I planned it accordingly. Surreptitiously he worked away, making a tool that provided tension to the four locking tumblers. Nowadays, you can buy these off eBay. Back in the day, they were harder to come by. Once he had picked it, up and could repeatedly do it, we made a date to climb the bell tower. The problem was, when could we do it without being caught?

There were Victoria College workmen walking around all day. There were regular gardeners, residence maintenance men, and the cleaning ladies. There was even a Porter, who never seemed to be in his office, where he was needed, but walking about. Watching them to try and determine their schedules made us feel as though we were prisoners of war in a camp. We decided on a Sunday afternoon, Easter Weekend.

I was guard, standing in the middle of the gate's entrance, with a good view in all four directions of the quadrangle, and signalled to

Carbonel when the coast was clear. Carbonel squirted in WD40 ('penetrating oil,' my Dad had called it, just mixed gasoline and machine oil), and the lock opened like a charm. Like guilty school children, we climbed the winding stairs; it was dark, pitch black, and it took time for our eyes to adjust. As a child, my father had taken me up Sir Isaac Brock's Tower – my mother was too fat to follow – and suspense builds as you climb the tower as you cannot see around the disappearing corners. What was it about corners? You want to know how long the stairs climb; you are always anticipating the end of the climb – but it goes on and on. The tower had been built to celebrate Sir Isaac Brock's victory of a few British regulars, some local farmers, and loyal natives – most natives fled to Canada after the American Revolution, as they knew they were going to get a better deal from the Crown – over the Americans at the Battle of Queenston Heights. But there had been narrow windows in the tower at Queenston – not here. Besides my hands on the cold walls, as we climbed, I could only feel the thick dust beneath my thin-soled shoes.

As we neared the top, light illuminated written messages by our hands. Faded but legible, there were the names of men signing up for the RCAF and going off to war. We added our names on the wall. This was yet to prove another of my poor judgment decisions. I think we were the first up there since WWII. It was a huge room; darkness claimed the height. There, in the middle, was a small bell on rough timber cradle and yoke. It said "Whitechapel Bell Foundry, London, 1913" – the same guys that made the Liberty Bell.

I had planned to have sex with him here; he had not anticipated my thoughts. I took the lead, fumbling with his pants. I lost my virginity by the bell and its dust, illuminated with the slanting light from the louvers of the tower windows. It had seemed, at first, like entering an Egyptian tomb with its warm and dank air. It took weeks, it seemed, to get the dust out of my long hair, the splinters out of my bum, and for the bleeding to stop. But it was loads of fun, and it felt great to have a man inside me. I had loved the feel of his hands on my breasts, and how he had had no idea how to undo the bra clasps. I felt thoroughly naughty and rebellious, revelling in the fact it had been my idea entirely. My roommate Ann had given me the condom. It was Easter Sunday, and now I might be pregnant. Shit.

Six months of my careful, detailed planning to seduce Carbonel Luna – the dark, handsome boy from a cattle rancher family outside of San Carlos on the Llanos – and I was reduced to a Jezebel, about to die, or get pregnant – same thing – from some condom filled with "sticky love juice," the typical third-rate romance (or was it porn?) book would say. But it was still sticky and nasty. I might as well jump from the tower to be eaten by stray dogs….

"I love you," I said unconvincingly. "It was great. You were great". I had no idea if he were good or not. All I knew was that I had dusted up my nose and what seemed to be splinters in my bum. And it hurt down there. And he weighed a lot.

I had spent months planning the adventure. I had seen the locked door with its cruciform lock. I knew Carbonel would want to pick the lock. He was dark, foreign, exotic, wealthy, and good-looking. Quiet, he also had a wry and subtle humour. He was going to be a dentist, he said. I wanted him. He was everything my father wasn't.

"You know, I bet before the boys went away to the War, they carved their names and addresses on the wall beside the bell with the date and the name of their sweetheart," I had foretold.

"Ja?" Carbonell had looked up from his book on Paediatric Orthodontics. I wanted him in the bell tower – picking the lock was only the start. I had to get him up the stairs. How many other girls had been there with their boyfriends, I wondered? Could I get him up the narrow stairs?

"Yup, it is the Canadian thing to do. We could add our names, too." I wove the story.

"O.K., we'll do it."

Once up there, I could place his hand on my bosom…I knew he looked at them – they were large. I had it all planned. And now, with the condom lost somewhere inside me, of course, I was likely pregnant. Loser Helen, the story of my life.

Luckily, I did not get pregnant. I felt like a fool at the clinic; by the time I saw the doctor, the condom had come out on its own. But it was awful waiting for the pregnancy test results.

While I was at the clinic, and boys being boys, Carbonel had spent the rest of that day with his buddies in his residence at South House (located, surprisingly, it might seem, south of Gate House) carrying paraphernalia of levers, extension cords, a quarter horsepower electric motor, reduction gears, two by fours and an alarm clock up the narrow winding stairs of the bell tower to assemble what would prove to be an outstanding prank. As the King James Version says, "when it was yet dark," on Easter Monday morning, the alarm went off, the motor started, the gears rotated, and the bell began to ring continuously all day across the Victoria College quadrangle. A veritable reminder of the Resurrection from the empty bell tower. Bong, bong, bong, bong, bong, it unceasingly clanged – but none of their workmen had keys to the tower. I could hear it clearly in my residence in Annesley Hall, two blocks away. The fact that the bell rang all day was perhaps the best part of it all. Carbonel and his buddies must have been rolling on the floor as a cabal of workmen stared at the WWII vintage cruciform lock and had no idea how to gain entry to the tower. It was an extremely loud and irritating sound! I couldn't think of a better prank.

I was still spotting when I walked over to the meeting with the Dean, a few days later, to meet this sour man with no sense of humour. I remember thinking, as I walked over to the New Academic Building, of both my fear of what he would say and do, as well as my clumsy fumbling with the slippery condom on Carbonel's eager and throbbing penis. Yes, I had discovered sex....

The worst part was that I had already had a run-in with the Dean. Well, it was not so much a run-in in that the University had made a mistake and was unable to say "sorry" to me, and, at the time, I had exploded. I received two scholarships, one from the University of Toronto and one from Victoria University, (a college of U. of T). Despite their fat salaries, numerous administrative clerks and a surfeit of bosses and processes, and a total lack of real work for them to do (all highlighted at the time in a series of articles in The Globe and Mail). Apparently, they were not able to co-ordinate full scholarships amongst themselves, and I had received two letters confirming both, when in fact, they meant to send only one. When I had gone in September of my first year to pick up two cheques, I had only got one. More on this story later.

"Helen Clark, you are aware of the cacophony, the pain, and the distraction to studies on Monday caused by the Gate House bell ringing all day?" he began.

"Well, it would have been hard not to hear it, Mr. Stokes."

"Helen, I have a copy of what your roommate says is your handwriting, posted on the message board at Annesley Hall," (here he passed my note that I had posted in the laundry room about my missing, much-loved sock with smiling pussy cats – it would by typical if my roommate, that twit Ann, had given him the note or ratted on me) "and am wondering why your name in what appears to be your handwriting is written in the Bell Tower. Would you know anything about that, Miss Clark?"

"Yes, I am still missing the matching sock," I replied.

"The writing on the wall is dated Sunday," he continued, ignoring me.

"Yes, I wrote on the bell tower wall on Sunday," I confessed.

"So, after you had broken into private property and defaced the wall, you set up a dangerously wired electrical motor?"

"Actually, I had nothing to do with the subsequent prank."

I never told him about the name next to mine on the wall, that of George Smallwood, who had served in 419 Squadron, RCAF. I researched it. He and his crew were killed laying mines at Skaggerak, Norway, on Easter Monday, April 25th, 1943. Late at night, in fog, his Halifax's low-level attack ("gardening" in R.C.A.F. parlance) likely hit the water. He and his crew never saw their families again - let alone the bell tower he had written his optimistic epigraph on two years earlier. But I know George would have laughed at the prank; he joined at 19, got his wings at 20 in Brantford, and was pilot of a crew a year later. What it must have meant to be 21 years old and responsible for a crew of seven over enemy territory in the middle of the night, with searchlights, shrapnel, and Schraege Musik fighters hunting you. He and his family had lived at 31 Keewatin. I later walked past the house – which is now shadowed by monstrous soulless concrete apartment blocks. Yet I sensed the house remembers; it had a history.

Carbonel had dropped me immediately. Curious, decades later, I searched for him on the internet; I found out he had drowned while scuba diving in the Maldives. A watery grave for him, too – though maybe not so cold.

Ai-Khanoum, 150 B.C.

Here's a challenge for you. Can you keep dreams and your day-to-day activities going at the same time? Will you be able to follow my stories – both dreams and real life? I am going to tell you about some of my dreams. Sometimes I wonder what reality is and what is an illusion. I have always had vivid dreams. I don't know what other people's dreams are like, but sometimes I remember mine, and I try to continue them the next night and the nights after that by adding people, events, and circumstances. If I am bored (I often was at school) and have nothing to do, I weave the story during the day, too. Usually, it works. I love jumping from one world to another – especially a private one in my mind.

These dream-stories become a mixture of the random unexplainable "bizarreness" of a regular dream with added bits by me. There is nothing supernatural or science fiction about them – but I do find them fascinating and unexpected. They seem to make the story up as they go along. I think Gombrich wrote the greatest book on art in the 20th century in his 'Art and Illusion.' He talks about how the artist changes what he or she sees – and, anyway, the reality you see or understand may not be the same as what the artist sees. Thus, we have perceptions or levels of illusions and reality – which is which? Reality, what the artist sees, or what you see? I want to share some of mine with you. Some of them seem to have prefigured or echoed events of my life – or is it my memory now twisting what I really believed then?

I remember walking back from the infamous meeting with the Dean about the prank (in the end, they could do nothing, and I like to think I triumphed as they realized I no longer feared them), past the blooming forsythia bushes by the front of the bell tower of Gate House, and of revisiting my then long-running Graeco-Bactrian dream. I think this dream started after reading about Alexander the Great and his protracted three-year war in Bactria and Sogdiana. Part of the excitement I had is for this story's exotic and far-off nature – this isn't the Battle of Hastings in AD 1066 or D-Day in 1944 that we all know – this was somewhere most of us don't know. Alexander had founded cities everywhere – Alexandria in Egypt being the most famous one today. The one I was dreaming about was Alexandria on the Oxus – Ai-Khanoum – effectively the furthest east Alexander would go and leave a major mark. Here is the map, rather the worse for wear, that I made at the time instead of listening to a lecture on the Italian humanist Ficino (whom I do NOT like as he misrepresents the Classical tradition):

Bactria then must have been a beautiful, rich, and fertile valley surrounded by high mountains, a resting point for the trade caravans of the Silk Road. All the kings and khans – Persian, Greek, Scythian – wanted to own Bactria. The dream had developed with grand sweeps of plains, of mountains, of rivers of the Hindu Kush, of fierce, unending wars, and the incongruity of Greeks building a theatre, a gymnasium, and yet another city, at the confluence of the Oxus and Kokcha rivers, so far from their ancestral homes and way of life. I let my imagination run rampant and thought of Bactria's thousand golden cities, of the incalculable mined wealth of copper, lead, iron, rubies, and the source of lapis lazuli! Ah, lapis lazuli, that intense, deep-blue, king of kings, jewel of my heart!

I am Greek, Queen Cleopatra Thea, in Ai-Khanoum, and as per custom, married to my brother (being a child growing up in the Methodist-Presbyterian prudishness of Canada, the thought of marriage and sex with my brother was, well, both bracing and dangerous) and the Saka invasion has begun – which will wipe out my land, my city, my family and a way of life….I am not sure how much was dream and how much I added, but I liked being carried away to another world – one that was doomed. It certainly whiled away boring lectures. Ai-Khanoum was a world within a world, now completely lost, on the very edge of the conquered world of Alexander. And so far from the Toronto of today.

I do remember thinking, as I walked under the tower, past the bright blooming forsythia, back to the red brick of Annesley Hall, of photographs of the archaeological dig I had seen of the unbaked bricks of my palace, of the peristyle (decorated courtyard) of 180 Corinthian columns, its ornate mosaic floors, its palmettes antefix (a fan of palm leaves of stone mounted on the edge of the roof covering the joints of tiles), and of its view from my citadel of the encircling mountains tipped with snow, and of the smells and sounds of the pack animals in the market in the city below. I wish I were a better artist to draw that scene for you. It must have been amazing. From the ruins excavated, even the palmettes antefix were stunning. They are unique winged palm leaves, splayed open, and there would have been hundreds of them placed around the frieze of my palace, just below the roof, with the wings ascending above the roof's edge. Another fine discovery was a votive plate of the goddess Cybele, drawn in a chariot by pair of lions! There was a mystical cult of the Phrygian goddess Cybele at Ai Khanoum, but as a Greek, I liked the regular gods of the Greeks...

Then I compared that rich and wide expanse of Ai Khanoum to the quiet stillness of the limestone blocks of the Men's Residence at Victoria College...with its dull and dirty flagstones.

Taliska, 1977

"I want you to meet him. He is an enormous teddy bear! I want to just hug him! And he likes me!"

"Sounds as though you are already in love" I smiled to Taliska de Catanzaro as we sat in Wymilwood, the student centre and meeting point of Victoria College. "How and where did you meet him?"

"He's from Brazil. His father works in a mine in Belo Horizonte, just as mine used to, up in Sudbury".

"What is he taking?"

"Oh, he's not at school – he is driving a truck for the Toronto Star. He is going to open a restaurant when he has saved enough money."

"Where did you meet him?"

"On my street – my books fell out of my bag as I was shutting the door, and they all fell down the stairs, and he was walking by, delivering a paper…"

"How convenient!" I teased, and Taliska continued: "…he helped me pick them up. It's true, and he's coming her today, now, in fact." She looked at her watch. "My mother likes him, too."

"He moves quickly." He had already met her mother, and her Mum speaks no English? "Did he learn to speak Italian in Brazil, too?" Taliska was a short girl with curly black hair, and she was going to have none of my teasing. Taliska was always no-nonsense and very serious.

"No, of course not, only Portuguese, but his English is good, and my mom was pleased to see him picking up the books for me." Just then, Taliska looked up and beamed.

"Helen, I'd like you to meet Adur Aquino; Adur, this is Helen Clark." Adur was huge. 6' 5" and thick. Taliska was dwarfed. They were both overflowing with smiles. A little bird in a giant gentle hand.

"Your initials are A.A.?" I raised my eyebrows and looked at Taliska - I had had to sober her up before she could go home to see her parents after a party at the start of school. Drinking was the rite of passage into university life – at least back then, it was.

"Oh, stop it, Helen!" she complained. I stood up, and we shook hands rather formally. Adur, rather sweetly, I thought, just kept smiling.

"Look, I have brought you some wild strawberries! I got them at the market!" Excitedly, Adur opens a bag of tiny little strawberries….

***

Soon, Adur and Taliska were joined at the hip, and Taliska dropped out of school for a lifelong love affair. They were lucky to have found each other. Eventually, they did open a restaurant together on Queen St., and it was a great success. Before we leave this vignette of happiness, I want to recount a memory with Taliska, that paragon of hard work, dedication, and single-mindedness.

Victoria College is the oldest of the colleges of the University of Toronto, if you are not familiar with them, and Old Vic is the old, central building of the college, sitting amidst a quadrangle of academic buildings – with a clear view of the Men's Residences, the infamous Gate and South Houses amongst them. It was late September when you feel the late morning's coolness burning off; the leaves are yellowing, crisping in the autumn air, the grass is green, and the birds have gone. I particularly liked how the ivy would turn purple that stretched across and around the grand gothic windows of Burwash Hall. We were sitting on the cold stone steps of Old Vic in the quadrangle, under the inscribed words upon the lintel, in the bold Roman font of old, "THE TRUTH SHALL MAKE YOU FREE." Actually, to this day, I still believe John 8:32's epigram is true.

"Taliska, it was lovely being invited to your home; thank you so much."

"Aww, it was nice having you! My parents loved you; they loved that you know so much and have opinions on everything…"

"Well, your childhood isn't the childhood that I had. Adur is a dreamer."

"We need dreamers. I WANT to believe in dreams." (Ah, I wonder what Adur and Taliska would have thought of my dreams?)

***

The door had opened, and Adur was already there. People were shouting, even screaming, in Italian at each other – probably about the weather or where the bowls should go on the table – but it was all so LOUD and unintelligible to me. And so unlike what I was used to. Adur was busy helping put chairs around the table, and I did not know anyone other than Taliska and Adur. I remember the Dad welcoming me with open arms and huge hugs, saying "Mangiacake" (a gentle insult to non-Italians, "a cake-eater"). It was all so open, sincere, and friendly. He could speak English well enough but probably preferred to revert to his Calabrian dialect. He was from Salento, on the Italian heel.

When I spoke to him later (to make conversation when he had sat beside me but had said nothing for a while) of the Byzantine Greek influence on Salentino (the local dialect there), he looked at me as though he had seen a ghost! (Be kind to me; I was young and talked about the things I liked, and I didn't realize you changed the conversation for your audience). A lovely, white-haired man, he had worked hard in the mines up north, and then he got himself a great job with a pension with CP Rail in Toronto. His family was everything to him. Mrs. de Catanzaro was still working feverishly in the kitchen, from where aromas of basil and tomato wafted in. When she wasn't in the kitchen, she was working in a knitting mill with a gaggle of other Italian women, saving for tomorrow and their children. Life's objectives were clearer then. Come to think of it, have life's objectives really changed? Of course, you work for your children…what else is there?

At dinner, Adur opened up. "Canada is the greatest country in the world." He did rather like to hold forth; Taliska revelled in it. "You don't know how lucky you are here. You even have a land registry office. Where I come from, you never know if you own the land you've bought. The cops are crooks. You bribe them. You bribe them to hunt for whoever robbed you; you bribe them to leave you alone. I missed a stop sign today, and I got a ticket. When I said I can't drive for the company with a ticket – he asked me when my probation was up, and when I said in a couple of months, he said it would take three months or more for the ticket to show up on my record. He was working with me – doing his job but helping me! We had slaves in Brazil until less than a hundred years ago; people still want slaves there in Petrópolis – that is where the rich people live, just north of Rio – even today! Here, you have mail delivered to your house every day! You have good government! And it is such a big, expansive country! There is no limit to what you can do! The British set you up with laws – and people obey them. People even WANT to obey them! In Brazil, laws are just a cost of doing business – you pay a bribe to get around them."

I had interjected. "It has been said, 'in the Developing World, time has no value, and neither do promises and words. Daily life is corruption, greed, lack of law, or any clear system to work within'". I don't think they got it, so I thought to myself, you might as well be hung for a sheep as a lamb, and continued, "…but Rome was great, too, with laws, Cincinnatus selflessly defending the traditions that built a great country, and then it fell apart with Nero, Caligula, who trampled on all the good of Rome. The price of freedom is eternal vigilance. Always the few will steal power and control from the many. Canada is great, but we need to keep an eye on the ball, or we will have 1984."

"Canada has free elections – we have army coups in Brazil! Canadians are educated. They can think. They will never have a corrupt government, with small interest groups pushing their own agenda!" retorted Adur.

(Ah, well, I wonder if Adur would still be so naïve today, all these years later).

***

"I had a happy childhood, Helen. You didn't?" asked Taliska, always the one to complete the loop, the circle, to think of others.

"No, Taliska. My parents either hated me – or were jealous of me. It wasn't indifference. They undermined me. I wished to be a man growing up. Men had more adventures! Real men led, had opinions and changed the course of history. I used to go to the library to read and read everything, just to escape. I wanted to be Boadicea or Cleopatra – someone who did things, not some sucky girl with pigtails having babies, wanting, and seeking love. I wanted to be a man. To lead, to make a difference. Not like my Dad, who never did anything. I wanted something more. I did not hate my parents. Can you hate what gave you life?"

A Sapling, 1972

I was frightened of high school. It was with great trepidation I entered the halls of Riverside High School. My imagination always ran ahead of me. I took Classical Greek, as it was held at lunch. This would mean I would not go home to lunch of a boiled hotdog and face my mother. There was that sickening residue of scum floating on the water after you took the limp, warm sausage out. With the heat off, the water calmed - yet that greasy film was still there, floating...the rest of it was in your stomach. That water always reminded me of my mother; after you finished whatever you were doing, there was something left behind of her that you did not want to see, feel or hear and yet could not escape. God, I hated that shit floating on the water.

I could not stand the fact we did not study the Classical Greek accent. The textbook had whole chapters on it. It was clearly essential, and we were not learning it. In ancient times music was everywhere; you could see that from all the musical instruments on their vases...and poetry was spoken out loud. So the accent was essential. We skipped the chapters. To listen to Homer, you must recite out loud; merely as a written language, you were losing half the effect. What was the purpose of reading about black sails before Troy, riding the wine-dark seas, if you could not listen to the waves breaking beneath the bronze ram, the crack of the canvas filling with Aeolian wind, the proud and yet cuckolded King of Sparta upon the prow, seeking my namesake? The teacher said it was too hard. Now

I think he did not know it himself. Spoken English cannot match the prosody of grand dactylic hexameter, the apex of poetic Western civilisation's metre...but what good things are not difficult? Dactylic hexameter is a metre that is ideal for grand epics, noble heroes, horrifying betrayals, and its predicable "beat" of long-short-short, long-short-short sounds gives a pattern that ties the poem altogether. The Aeneid starts out: 'arma virumque canō, Troiae quī prīmus ab ōrīs., so it would be read out loud as 'ARma virUMque caNO, TROIae qui PRImus ab ORIS. It doesn't work in English, as English has many more unpredictable polysyllables. "I sing of man and the arms, who, exiled by fate, first came from the coast of Troy to Italy..." And of course, back then, all the stories were known by the listeners, the poems were memorized, and were sung out loud to an audience....poetry was taken seriously in those days. Great, moving stories require effort. Great events lead to suffering. Suffering leads to art. The appreciation of art transcends the mediocre because it requires effort and critical thinking...

I am sure I was an insufferable classmate, but I was in my own world, happy and unaware of what others thought. Here is a poem that I wrote:

Choices Made

As a child, I dreamed of sun-bleached, salt-crusted Odysseus,
Washed naked onto the beach,
And succoured by the diaphanous-clothed Nausikaä.

Lying on the bed, my head cupped in my hands,
I would see Alcinous in his hall;

Hear the citharis play, the clatter of plates,
The sounds of eating and drinking.
Repeated toasts and stories of wondrous places,
Dogs fighting over scraps; fussing babies and servants' feet.

The ceiling is high; clothes are rich;
Gold and sculptured ceramics crowd the tables.
And rolls of wafting smells of roasted food.

But most of all I saw Nausikaä; dark-haired,
Sitting by her father's side; beautiful; quiet.
Nausicaa of the white arms.
Who could leave her?
Independent, strong-willed, brave, yet obedient.
I loved her.

Nausikaä, I cried for you when Odysseus left.
Did you watch his ship slip from its birth?
Did he scan the shore, his hand shielding his brow, as the ship ran
With the tide and the morning eastern sun?
He was the cunning one; the wily one.
He would not tarry.

They say Telemachus, though, came to you.
Ah! To have Telemachus come for me in a swift-running ship,
Across the rolling seas.

If I couldn't be Odysseus and change the world, then I would
be a Nausikaä and save the world by saving his life on the beach.
But actually, Nausikaä didn't do much. I really wanted to be Hector.
He was brave, fighting for a lost cause, knowing he was doomed to
die (shit, like all of us!), yet strong enough to support his wife and
child – and hide his coming doom. And who can forget that passage?
After kissing farewell to his wife Andromache, he bends down to
hug and kiss his child, and his plumed helmet frightens the child,

who bursts out in tears! Surely this is the greatest passage in literature of all time? The noble father, doing what he can to protect his family, never fearing his duty, knowing he is going to die, is thwarted by an innocent child's fear of the tools of war and death! It does not get better than that. That is why it has survived; these days, we forget the title of last year's winner of the Governor General's prize, let alone the plot…

Come to think of it, Andromache (whose name means 'fighter of men') stands out as a symbol of virtue and fidelity, an example of the suffering of the Trojan women and all who suffer in war. She is carried off by Achilles' son to Epirus, where she continues the funeral offerings to Hector. Eventually, she becomes Queen of Epirus, and her son founds Pergamon, that famous city where she eventually dies. Thus, noble deeds are shared by all the Greeks and are used to spread more founding myths…and the common inheritance binds all. Yes, there was a time when high moral principles and ideals were a noble aspiration. Who are our heroes today? We are too busy pulling them down, I'm afraid.

Well, I would prefer to hear about brave deeds and altruism. Today, we only talk about the failures and weaknesses of our more recent founders. And then it is rather a selective list of those we are allowed to consider heroes. Hector lived for something larger than himself – an ideal. Today, we live for ourselves. Civilizations die when they cannot think of others. Carthage, in effect, died because its greedy merchants shipped grain to Rome while Hannibal campaigned outside its walls.

But it wasn't only romantic dreams and visions of long-lost loves and wars of yesteryear that carried me through the long corridors of Riverside High School. Mathematics fascinated me. Another book that I found in the basement was Mathematics for the Millions, published in the 1930s. Its yellow pages cracked and sometimes broke as I turned its pages. I don't know whose book it was – was it my Dad's? Or my Mum's? As a child in the basement, I was fascinated by how to determine the height of a mountain from miles away with geometry, to determine the escape velocity required from the earth's gravity, and to gauge the age of the universe by measuring the sun's moving shadow upon the ground. Well, yes, I am trying to put too much into one sentence for effect. But mathematics pulls it all together.

Was it Einstein who said the pencil was smarter than he, as it carried him somewhere else? There are only two types of activities in life – everything can be reduced to either a kind of stamp collecting or applied mathematics. Everything substantial is based on mathematics. Physics, Latin, and Greek are examples of applied mathematics. Either you get it, or you don't. Physics is both how you understand reality and the effect of your imagination on this reality. Physics is about organic patterns of energy. And passion. Plato really summed it up; the smallest things are not physical objects in the ordinary sense; they are forms or ideas. This comes clearer in quantum mechanics – as Newtonian physics can't describe it all. Clearly, we can't live in a romantic dream. But the fact that pure numbers alone don't answer it all leads to a much bigger question. The answer to the universe is not 42 – as the famous hitchhiker suggested. That is just not satisfactory. The mere fact that the answer to the Ultimate Question of Life, the Universe, and Everything, is actually now a joke reflects how we have given up. But we want answers! Part of the answer lies in merging, or the understanding, of everything at the same time – the Apollonian, the Dionysian, and how they interrelate, was Thomas Mann's answer. The secret is appreciating all the components – all at the same time. We will get there. The journey itself is the answer, as we are mortal, and mathematics, coupled with our Unknowns and Unknowables, pulls it all together. Everything is just not simple. But we DO want to know! We are all seeking something.

There is a grand scheme – from the first cry of a newborn baby to the unexplainable, unmeasurable, unknowable, unbelievable expanse of the universe. How it all fits together is a journey that I am only now beginning to understand. We may have a shorter journey or a longer one. Mine, though, always seems to have been troubled.

Returning to high school, we had to sign up for sports in gym class. As I had no interest in exercise, I avoided the sign-up lists for as long as I could. Finally forced, I signed up as the Khan Brothers; Genghis Kahn for volleyball, Aga Khan for ice hockey, and Ali Khan for basketball. Others didn't think me funny; of course, I could not even skate! They thought I was weird. Of course, it was weird! But it was also absurd and funny. Too few have a sense of irony. Humour is indeed part of the journey. We need to STRETCH.

Strange thing is that my gym teacher went out of her way to be understanding and kind to this social misfit who couldn't catch a ball. I did try. The ball deliberately hit my fingers and bent my fingers the wrong way, and it hurt like hell. Fucked if I was going to play basketball. Why couldn't they use a soft volleyball in basketball? The fact is that teachers were kinder to me than they should or could, have been. The strangest lesson for me is that I did not appreciate the allowances they made for me. Maybe the teachers were tolerant of differences – or they were lucky and had already found the meaning of life I so desperately sought then – or then again, perhaps I did not know what I was searching for.

But I was safe at high school. I hadn't spread my wings and destroyed myself. Or I didn't understand that all the book learning isn't necessarily going to help you in life. But might it help? The problem was joining, combining, getting the overview, and finding the balance…the golden mean. To me at the time, and even today, the issues and complaints of my 'teenage years' growing up seemed to pale beside the larger issues of 'life'…God, no wonder why my classmates gave me a wide berth. What on earth did they think of me in my own cloud? Can I learn the conjunction of love, place, and memory, even now?

My memories are a series of vignettes for me. Back in the early 70s, families kept their secrets. My mother beat me; I had bruises on my legs when I went to school. I thought it normal. Now I can't think why she hit me. Was she jealous of me? Did she think it was normal to hit your kid? Was she just unhappy with her life and took it out on me? Or was she a directionless, confused, and wandering lost soul, just as I would become? I don't know. My parents did not want me to escape to the University of Toronto – whether on a scholarship or not. They seemed to do everything to hold me back.

Riverside High School had a great music programme; I would linger by the Music room and listen to sublime music drifting out before heading home. Walking out onto Princeton Ave., looking north to the distant Gatineau Hills, listening to Chopin repeating in my head, I would be transported to imagined Viennese streets, gaslights, overcast skies, drawing rooms, men in dark suits, and women in long dresses…it was all so long ago, and so much better than my life…

The branches of the ginkgo tree outside our house had minds of their own, growing and hanging down as they (independently) chose, like long, loose strands, gently swaying in the breeze. Their serrated triangular leaves flickered in the breeze, slowly oblivious to the world around them. Their greenness was so brief.

Father had a bronze-riveted, wooden-handled knife with a leather sheath that he said he had been given to him by Lord Baden Powell. He even had a faded picture of him as a young lad with Baden Powell at some Boy Scout awards ceremony. He said he got it for his work with rough city boys at Roland House in Bethnal Green, London, England, before the war. He treasured it. One day he had used it to parge the wall and had not cleaned it. The next day, he struggled and struggled to clean it but could not remove all the mortar. He would look at it and have this sense of loss, failure, and disappointment in his eyes that I will never forget. He had that same look when I asked him about the war. There were books to treasure in those eyes if you could reach them. What had he been through? He never told me. Or I should have asked.

My mother was different. "I hate you!" My mother was raging at me while I mentally escaped to the cold world of icicles outside. This, of course, may have made her rages worse. Only those that have grown up in Ottawa know what winter is about. The bitter, bright, blinding, cold. Green ginkgo leaves were only a brief interlude in the overlong hell of Ottawa winters.

I remember looking at the sunlight shining through the icicles at our house in Ottawa while my mother raged. I was in the sitting room, looking out over the front steps. The sun glistened in a thousand little baby suns reflected all the way down the icicle – every half inch or so, there was a decrease in its diameter, like transparent tyres on top of each other – and a little sun shone through each one. It was beautiful and magical. Each icicle would drip at its own rate, oblivious to the world around it.

"I hate you." She repeated. Did she really mean it? Can you really hate your daughter? Or was it just a word to use? Well, sometimes she did, and sometimes she didn't. Growing up, it seemed to be most of the time; she wanted me good as dead. It was horrible. I had to escape, but you can't as a child. And in those days, you didn't talk about problems at home when you were at school.

You were alone. But maybe to my mother, I was her, reincarnated again in a carbon copy of herself, growing up, and she resented looking at herself again? She was bright; maybe she, too, had not "fitted in," and her mother had hit her, too? Maybe I was a symbol of her own perceived failures and the easiest thing to take revenge on?

My earliest memories are of my mother screaming at – and sometimes hitting – my father while my father, a slim, fragile man, sat quietly in his wing chair. They are awful memories. He should have hit her back. But her worst rages were at me.

"I wish you were never born!" she would yell. Most people have baby pictures. There are none of me. An only child, I must have been a mistake. Of course, these days, I wouldn't have been born at all. I would have been sucked out and chopped up. Maybe they would have sold my baby's organs to make vaccines - or worse. Frankly, I can't even imagine my Dad making love to my mother.

Him, small and thin, pounding my large and thick mother, missionary position? Maybe I wasn't his child: there's a thought! My mother had been pretty. But now she was large and a monster.

A Seedling, 1968

"No."

"Yes, you are!"

"No, I'm not."

"You'll do as you are told."

"You can't make me!"

This was the start of my rebellion against her and the harbinger of hell for me. And it was at the age of 10. It was all downhill from here.

"I am leaving your father, and you are coming with me." My father didn't make enough money for her, and my mother was leaving him.

"No, I am staying with Dad."

We were in the car, sitting in the parking lot at Carlingwood Shopping Centre. It was one of those large open malls where you parked miles from two big stores and a collection of connected smaller stores and walked and walked, in the cold Ottawa winter, to an open but covered concrete path, between stores, freezing. Your toes were frozen in your boots which were themselves covered with salt and ruined with those white stains.

It was at university that I learned about Dante's frozen hell. Dante understood the cold of Ottawa! A fiery hell is demonic anger and laughter – like my mother. It has emotion. Ottawa has iciness and silence, a different kind of hell, a worse hell than heat. Frigidity and separation. Silence. Ottawa did not talk to me. Dante's hell has Satan immersed in ice; the sinners in the ninth circle of hell have forsaken the bonds between themselves and others; they repudiate what it means to be human and cannot communicate. To me, growing up, Ottawa was immersed in a block of ice, a soulless place of indifference and self-interest. There is no absolution from the Ottawa cold.

And the days were always short. It seemed to be dark all the time. When you got up, it was dark; when you were coming home from school, it was dark. The only relief from the cold was sitting in a car, with the heater noisily blowing hot, dry air. And, more often than not, in the car, I had my mother telling me what to do.

"Scott Mortimer is getting a divorce, and I am marrying him."

"Go ahead," I said, staring at the huge Loblaws sign and the dark figures shuffling miserably to their cars.

"I am moving in with him."

"I'm staying with Dad."

She didn't. And why would she want to take me if she hated me, anyway? It just did not make sense to me. But she never forgave me. We drove home in silence, and father was sitting in his chair, watching TV. Scott Mortimer was some type of insurance adjuster who made lots of money. He had a big Chrysler. When the windows were down and you opened the door, there was no window frame on the door. So, when the window was up, this thin piece of glass was sticking out on top of this monstrously large, 200-pound heavy steel door – it was just incongruous, out of proportion. It looked as though a tank could hit the door and do nothing to it, and just touching the naked thin glass with your finger could break it. So much of the commercial world seems out of proportion; you need perspective, a place from which to observe and judge.

It was a very fancy car. I remember sitting in it; it had everything electric. He showed me the buttons, bragging about what they could do, from electric seats to automatic blow jobs. (Well, he told me everything was automated). He told me to press the buttons. So, I pressed them all at the same time, and the car stalled. He did look foolish and small as he panicked, trying to turn off all the fancy buttons. He did not like me from the first time I met him – and the feeling was mutual.

My father. What was Roland House? What had he done for the Boy Scouts, those rough city boys? Did he have passion as a child, idealism, and imagination? If so, where did it go? The desire to help, youthful ambition, the will to make a difference? Now his dreams were gone; he was old, utterly worn, and beaten. If only I had reached his soul!

Dad was a janitor.

I had one friend growing up. Sarah. She was very Jewish, very fat, and rather ugly. In fact, she was so fat she was totally round. I realize you are not supposed to say this today, but as children, we knew she was fat and ugly, and that is the way she was. Her father was NOT wealthy. His relatives never made it out of Dachau. He never forgot this, and this gave him humanity. He was different from other parents I knew. This humanity he passed onto his daughter, who was kind and loving. He sold ties at Joe Feller. He said standing behind the showcase showing ties gave him the confidence he needed to have to sell ties. His family had been tailors before the war, but there weren't any tailoring jobs in Ottawa. He said he couldn't go out there and sell insurance and brag like Scott Mortimer did.

I preferred Sarah's dad. He rather liked my childish banter. Sarah believed in truth, honesty, and standing up for what she believed in. She always knew what was wrong and what was right. I liked her. She didn't make fun of me. I wish I had not lost touch with her.

My mother had another side. She could be charming and get her way. It usually worked with policemen, teachers, and shop keepers. If you met my mother, you might think what a wonderful family we were. But we weren't.

I was a tomboy and ran with the local boys as a kid. What else was I to do? Stay in the house and be criticized by my mother? There were boys everywhere on the street when I was growing up. I was good at getting my way with them; it was easy to boss them around. I liked being their boss. I was often the ringleader, telling others to ring the doorbell of the poor old man next door and run away. Harmless annoying things, but still, it was a mean act overall. I have a mean streak, it is true. I created opportunities to do what I wasn't supposed to do. My comeuppance had yet to appear – indeed, it has lasted a lifetime.

I have a picture of myself with Santa at around age nine, and it is a very striking photo. I look very pretty – stunning, actually. I look very grown up, angelic, even. A beautiful, oval face. Perfectly proportioned and framed with gently curling, golden-brown hair falling down below my shoulders. The soft hair, well combed and lovingly arranged, frames my face. I don't remember the actual date – it must have been Santa's helpers who arranged my hair so nicely. The overall effect is rather haunting. I knew I looked good from an early age as I noticed the reaction people had when they met me. It was often embarrassing (but secretly gratifying).

Throughout my life, my good looks and intelligence have been a hindrance to me. You may think I am a self-centred, narcissistic, and self-destructive bitch. I hope, after reading about my life, you will think I am just an insecure girl that made a few – well, ok, many – poor decisions and didn't use her gifts wisely. I always wanted to belong and to be like everyone else. It is just that I achieved less than I should have, felt I was a charlatan, and, perhaps worse, was just plain lazy. Maybe most people are like this. In my case, though, I should not have tried to be something I wasn't. Now I think that was my mistake. By trying to be someone I wasn't, I gave up what I believed in and what I knew for something I neither knew nor understood.

I was born into an Ottawa lower-middle-class family, with a stay-at-home mother and a civil servant father, although we were poorer than most. My mother, Rebecca, was strong and wore the pants. My father, Ralph, went off to work, and then he came home. My mother went out to work as I grew up. My dad never seemed to be present. He would just watch television. He seemed to sit in his chair, literally, all day. I am not sure what he watched or even what he liked. Television just seemed so boring to me. He clearly loved my mother but never gave me what I think I needed – direction or support. I needed him, and he was never there for me. He was absent, off in his own world. I didn't know where to turn or who to talk to when I needed help. I didn't even know there was help out there. I dismissed him as unhelpful and useless. I had a lot to learn and didn't know it.

At the time, growing up, I thought him retarded. Maybe it was the foolishness of youth or just the self-centredness of the young, incapable of thinking of others. Slim, wiry, and healthy, Dad lived to 95. Now I wish I had talked to him and asked him more questions. I don't even know what he did in the war. But he never stood up to my mother. He never defended me. He enabled her treatment of me. He never talked to me. He never helped me. I suppose it is not surprising I didn't talk to him.

I had everything I needed, though. I knew then, and I know now, that others would have had less than I did. I didn't use what I had.

***

Curiously I loved my mother. She was the only mother I had. But she was cruel, selfish, and controlling. She crushed my spirit and tried to kill my passions and independence. I think she enjoyed crushing me. It was all about what she wanted. But, paradoxically, she also drove me to excel as a child. She wanted me to be the lawyer or doctor that she never was. And she nearly got what she wanted. I was in law school before I was 19 and had come first in the whole City of Ottawa in Latin, Greek, Physics, and Maths when graduating high school. I was even first violin in the Toronto Youth Symphony while doing my undergraduate degree at Victoria College...there were a lot of reasons for people not to like me. Yes, the highpoint of my life was early, and it was downhill from there. In hindsight, I had everything, did not know it, and then lost it all.

I especially remember how I enjoyed being the first girl to come first in Physics. Men teachers expected their chosen boys to win, but I beat them all. I am proud of that. I was quiet in class, but I never stopped thinking and reading. Well, that was then. Yes, I had everything going for me. I beat them at Physics even when I was more interested in being Perry Mason or Dr. Kildare. At that age, you DO want to please your mother. These would-be Physics winners in Grade 13 had only studied their textbooks and didn't understand that Aristotle's general discussions actually provided me an overview that helped with the details. And you had to read outside of the textbook. You needed the theory to understand the facts. You needed to see the forest as well as the trees. It DID help to understand the Platonic Forms, the "Nous." For my age, I was a polymath and had the looks to kill.

On top of this, I had large breasts and lovely legs. No one warned me that women don't like women prettier than them, though. Or that many nice boys are frightened of good-looking girls. Worse, I did not understand that intelligence can be a curse. It gave me a false sense of security. And intelligence doesn't mean you are going to be happy. Or that you make the right choices. In fact, being smart was detrimental to me. And I lost the very humility that I admired in Socrates… (But, come to think of it, didn't Socrates lose his intellectual humility himself in his own trial for his life? Maybe my readers will make allowances for me, too? We're all human).

My mother made me work at a young age – first at Simpson Sears and then at Armstrong and Richardson. I sold shoes. I hate shoes. They never did fit me. I would rather be reading, but I had to work selling things. In those days, I wore a short skirt (just as everyone did), so it was hard to be modest. I would wear white leotards so that white underwear would not be so noticeable when I had to bend for boxes. Of course, you would sit legs tightly together or both off to one side as much as possible, but it is still hard when you are measuring men's feet – and you have to be on your guard. It was not my fault my breasts developed early, too.

My mother was also lazy. I had to iron clothes and sheets for hours at a time. It seemed my entire weekend was spent ironing. I thought of Cinderella. I had to iron the dresses for her to go out with her lover. Oh, she looked nice when she went out. My mother could not cook, too. What she did cook was awful. She gave me the biggest pieces of fat, I swear. She made disgusting sausages that she had made in the sink. It literally was offal. Not only did it smell bad after cooking, but it also smelled bad raw. I have to assume she did not like to cook and not that she was trying to poison me. And the dirt on her countertop turned me into a sterilizing nut as I grew up.

She was from the Gorbals in Glasgow. Do you know what the Gorbals are or were? The Gorbals were possibly the worst slums in all of Europe. Once born into a slum-like that, it is hard to escape. Schools there were poor, opportunities non-existent, and crime rampant. And no one cared. It speaks volumes, of course, that my mother got out. She hitched herself to my dad, thinking he was going places. And compared to where she was from, he did. It is just that she wanted more. Even in the 1960s and 70s, I believe, privies were mostly outside in the Gorbals, coal was used for heat, and telephone boxes were on the street corner. I remember hearing a news story that my mum and dad talked about where apartment dwellers heard what they thought were dreadful explosions. The very building that they were in was shaking. They went outside to find the city council had decided to have some more slum clearance and had ordered what they thought was a derelict building to be knocked down. The wrecking ball was swinging. No one had checked to see if people were still living in the building. Hundreds were.

Ottawa is a soulless place. It was then. I am sure it still is, and it will always be so. And it is not just me saying this. Elizabeth Smart was the daughter of a wealthy Ottawa lawyer and a "socially significant wife." Smart grew up in a house next to William Lyon Mackenzie King, who would be the future Prime Minister in 1921. Smart was an outsider, a contrarian, devoted to literature, and a victim of her mother's hate. No wonder I liked her! Her most famous work, *By Grand Central Station I Sat Down and Wept,* written in anapaestic metre – those damned Greek feet again! LOL – tells of her affair with the poet George Barker and her three illegitimate children. She clearly loathed Ottawa and its insular, bourgeois respectability, which forbade her lover's entry to Canada. Her mother even ensured her book was banned and burned. You can't make this stuff up. Read Rosemary Sullivan's biography of her. Smart says, "Those who might have been poets go into External Affairs and never speak again. Ottawa is full of…snobbery and caution. It is a place to be pleasant and nothing but pleasant."

***

At a young age, I was walking everywhere. I remember walking, and walking, to Carlingwood Shopping Centre, to the doctor's, to the various schools I attended; it always seemed with heavy shopping bags, schoolbooks, and my violin. My mother liked to make me walk as she knew I hated walking. There is a loneliness to walking. I did not have a happy childhood. In those days, you didn't talk about your home life to anyone. I was lonely, ever so lonely.

It was cold in the winter; there were no sidewalks, and ice lived underfoot. Crunch, crunch, went your feet on the frozen snow when it was really cold. Your ears and nose froze, and on the coldest days, it hurt to breathe. Black ice was the worst. You did not expect it as you could not see it. All of a sudden, you slipped and were on the ground, and your parcels and shopping bag contents broken or dispersed on the hard black grit and dirty snow and ice. Oh, if you had money, you could enjoy winter and go skiing at Camp Fortune. But that was for the groovy set. They were all the beautiful people, and they didn't want to know people like us. People were generally unfriendly, and everything about the place was so narrow, so prescribed, so controlled, and mediocre. There was no imagination.

I even remember my violin teacher, a gifted Jewish lady from Winnipeg, commenting how unnatural Ottawa was. She said it was as bad as Ottawans were politicians, natural-born liars, rotating through Ottawa every four years with each election. I liked her as she said I was gifted. She only took advanced students but took me even though I was a beginner. My mother had shown up uninvited at a recital and cajoled her sufficiently so that she took me as a student. Even though I had not had lessons before that, I played something horrid on the spot, and she took me. I never looked back.

I tried to escape my mother all the time. She was always telling me what to do and that one day; I would support her. Dream on, honey. I had taught myself to read. If I were reading, I would get fewer jobs to do. At a very young age, I found a book in the basement about my namesake. It was not like the other books I had found (and read surreptitiously under the bedclothes, like her 'Valley of the Dolls'). This book was coffee-stained and dog-eared. Whose was it? My mother and father had both not finished high school – yet they had this book. The Queen in the story had been married but ran off with another man. I had thought I knew all about affairs, so my curiosity was aroused. The Queen's husband, weak like my father, asked his brother to help him get her back. They had weird and long names and lived long ago – and this added to the excitement of my far-off escape. What bothered me at the time, though, is that very little was said about my namesake, Helen. The story was really about her.

She was clearly beautiful, as her face had launched a thousand ships. My mother was pretty, too. Although they both had wimpy husbands, at least this ancient one had a brother who had balls. This brother was a king who could gather whole armies and then even sacrificed his own daughter, Iphigeneia, to get his brother's wife back! This was heady stuff for a little girl living in her own world. Imagine killing your own daughter so that the gods would let the winds blow – so you can start a war for ten years and kill more people? Sitting in the basement (it was a private place for me), I dreamed of being the famous Helen, desired and treasured by all. I also liked the brother of the husband. I wanted a man of presence, who commanded silence when he entered the room, who could lead men and then would devour me. Yes, my heart was stirred by Agamemnon. Agamemnon was not wimpy like my dad. At the time,

I didn't know about, or understand, what he did and what happened to him when he returned home to Mycenae...

Now I want to get to my first adventure. A school trip to Washington, D.C., had been organized for grade 8, and I was looking forward to it. With no surplus money, our family had not been out of Canada. Washington seemed exotic. I also read American books, American comics and listened to American music. It was not like to-day; it was hard to hate America. And let's face it: Ottawa is cold, smug, boring, and filled with navel-gazing, self-centred do-gooders and a never-ending circulation of self-serving politicians. Even at that age, I wanted out of the Ottawa Valley. I couldn't stand how they would say "fil-im" instead of "film."

Ottawa was so parochial, and every female had to have the same opinion – or you were ostracised. I wonder if it is still like that today.

A Day in the Life of Helen Clark, 1972

The teacher, Mr. Szabo, who organized the trip, was from Hungary. I wanted to go to Hungary. There had been a revolution there, and he had been able to escape. We never locked the door on our house, and I did realize how lucky we were in Ottawa. Ottawa was too boring to have revolutions. But strong views, violence, government torture, killing, and control stirred my heart with a sense of injustice that had to be righted. In that regard, I was a normal kid! I liked this teacher, as he was tall, slim, and good-looking. He also played the violin, playing Monti's Csárdás to the class and taking me to the ninth heaven with its haunting tune. I loved folk music; I would think of the countless towns, villages, and generation after generation of everyday people, gathering and listening to these ageless and eternal songs and tunes, laughing, loving, and living and dancing to timeless music. The music is timeless. I can still see him now and the vision he was trying to create. (Yes, now you see why I loved the folksongs Carbonel would sing of Venezuela and of its plains….)

He also had opinions – a rarity in west-end, bland, Ottawa. He thought it a good idea to show us a city where "the truth shall set you free," a bastion of independent justice, democracy and of ideals trying to exist in a "fallen" world of inequity and iniquity. Yes, I had a childhood crush on him. Who amongst you wouldn't? Best of all, he told me I could be Prime Minister one day. At the time, I did hold the dream he might like me the way I liked him, but of course, he was only encouraging me to work hard – and he had met my mother at parent-teacher interviews. He knew what I was up against. He was a leader and knew right from wrong. What better trip for young minds than to see Washington, where the ideals of the collective whole fought with the reality of selfish lobbyists?

I read all about the upcoming trip. I planned it all. I even wrote a poem about stopping in a small town on the way there:

Along the Susquehanna

We turned off the Interstate,
And delved down the snaking lines of road
To a forgotten town.

Here, beside old houses
Of long porches, tall windows, and long memories,
I walked to the graveyard.

Over the wet, cracked sidewalk,
Covered with leaves, flattened
By the cold, spitting March rain,

I saw a gnarled, black oak
Standing guard to an old cross
And its little sodden flag.

Into the General Store
I found what I knew I would find,
A kind old man helping a gentle, retarded man.

And I knew, and they knew,
What was important.
I love you, America.

I even imagined finding a gravestone in this overgrown cemetery inscribed with the epitaph of a wounded Unionist soldier who returned from the hellhole of the Andersonville prisoner of war camp only 'to linger a year before slipping away.' The gravestone would be weather worn, cracked, and touched with lichens and moss. I worked out all the details in my mind, down to the various weeds growing at the foot of the stone and the stone's kilter at fifteen degrees.

Like so much of my life, expectations of the trip to Washington did not materialize. Some parents, with suitably Waspish and French-Canadian names, decided that it was "unCanadian" to go to Washington and school children should visit Canada for the field trip. You know the type of parents they were. Rung-climbing civil servants, connected to the governing party, belonging to the right clubs, supporting the right charities, born to the right parents, and parroting the flavour of the week. Rich and comfortable, you knew they didn't know what suffering was and had never had a setback or a single disadvantage all their lives. What would they have known about the Hungarian secret police?

These know-it-all parents demand that you believe in what they believe – as they think they own the truth. They would drive $100,000 electric vehicles today and make fun of those who could not afford them. They are a different type of incarnation of my mother. So, these smart and learned people chose Moosonee for our school trip. I kid you not. Instead of a long bus trip through the heartland of America, down interstates, and through towns and valleys to the city of the most powerful, rich, and successful country in the world, we went on a slow, uncomfortable third-class train through neglected and forgotten towns, to the armpit of Canada. The misnamed Polar Bear Express stops in the middle of nowhere to pick up and drop off customers. In fact, at one town, the train did not stop where it normally stopped as the previous day drunks on the train had been thrown off, and they were frightened of more fights if they stopped! On our trip, all of those we picked up en route were drunk. It took us a day to get to Moosonee. Perhaps the slow speed of the train with its rhythmic rumblings helped the travellers to sober up.

The truth must be told, and that is that Moosonee is to be avoided. The highlight of the town is the liquor store. We arrived on the hottest day of the year, dressed in our parkas – as we had been told it would be cold. That year, on that day, it was the hottest place in Canada. This was our luck. The unexpected heat may explain why so many drunks were passed out on the street. Certainly, we were suffering as they were. Suffering animals are put out of their misery. If we had inspired leaders like Emperor Hadrian, the place would just be bulldozed, and he would start over. Hadrian was gay and had balls. He understood both the arts and the administrative needs of the Empire. But you are not going to find such inspired leadership in conformist, glib, and smug Ottawa.

Worse, on the day we arrived, I got the Curse. My first period and my curse of dysmenorrhea began. This affliction was to plague me for the next 30 years. Though I never had a child, I thought it was the worst pain imaginable. It was immobilizing. It debilitates. It destroys. The waves of cramps are the incoming, incessant tide. And like waves themselves, some cramps are bigger and worse than others; they just keep coming. The Curse. The unending pain. The first day of five. Every month.

That day will be forever marked for me. I had wormed my way into sitting beside the good-looking lad I liked. This David was intelligent in class and did not hang out unduly with what I called the "Seven-Up Crowd" those normal kids that were all friends were conformists, liked the same things, and did the same things, and wore the same clothing, etc. They went skiing together, were allowed to go to parties, were popular, etc. – everything I wasn't. Now I wanted to be David's friend. I had a heavy coat on, couldn't walk, talk, or even act as though I was interested in anything for the pain, but I had to act NOW to get the attention of the boy – or, as I clearly saw in my panic – never would I see another dawn, if I did not talk to David NOW….but what was I to say?

"David," I grimaced as another cramp seized me, "Would you like a toffee?"

"No thanks, Helen."

Then the worst rolled over me. Girls nearby had overheard my futile attempt at would-be friendship, and guffaws of laughter rang out as they circled me in my shame and failure. Jeering, they asked each other if they wanted toffees. They convulsed in laughter. My very own classmates betrayed me and revelled in my embarrassment. I do think girls can be crueller than boys. I felt like the 17th century natives, trying to welcome the Pilgrims with open arms their way by wearing skunk oil. Completely misunderstood, they had only convinced the Europeans that they were smelly savages and ignorant. Intentions are so often misunderstood. What did Gombrich say about misunderstanding communication, illusions, and each other's realities? My insides writhed in cramps, and my mind writhed in the horror of my failure; David walked off. He probably forgot about me that minute, and I never crossed his mind again. But it was to be the first signature mark of my many failures with the opposite sex. No wonder I wanted to change sexes. It was horrible being a girl.

At Cochrane, even the trees gave up. Until there, we had a grand view of lakes, rocks, and trees. And more lakes, rocks, and trees. It was a tad monotonous. They all looked the same. Upon arriving in Moosonee, not only were there no trees but there was also no station, either. It really was the end of the world. We climbed down and crossed the seasonal spring mud to a dilapidated bus. Did you know that in Moosonee, the Ontario Highway Traffic Act does not apply? You can't drive to Moosonee. You either come by train, air, or boat. Even the roads give out before you get there! We had left civilization behind. The bus had to make a few trips to take us all to school, where we were to sleep. We stood either in shallow puddles or on soft, wet ridges of mud churned by the bus waiting our turn. My feet got wet. Canada is brown, muddy, and unpleasant after the snow melts. This was May, a hot May day, and it was a Feast Day for the black flies. I could not believe the size of the bites they gainfully took. I suspect our sacrifices to the flies that day are still celebrated up there in the numberless miles of muskeg and breeding swamps of black and deer flies. After all, they had had a whole day to prepare their assault on us as our pathetic train had struggled over the desolation that is Northern Ontario.

You ask, what is there to do in Moosonee? There are no roads in or out. Someone asked the bus driver, and he replied gamely, "We have skidoos." (Oh God, the winter was all year long?)

He then proceeded to explain how they started them in the long, cold winters. "The men urinate upon the carburetors before cranking the engines." He luxuriantly said "urinate," stressing the first syllable and stretching the word out for as long as possible for maximum effect. Passing water is a special, holy, and enjoyable pastime in Northern Ontario. But with all the drinking, I guess a lot of time is spent peeing.

Luckily for us, the long yellow icicles we imagined were long gone. And how did women start them? Crouched over the carburetors? I didn't ask. But I did have some shopping to do. One young teacher – Mary Leka – must have noticed my discomfort, the frequent trips to the bathroom, and possibly the smell of my blood. Quietly, she explained about pads and belts and loaned me money.

Bless her. Guess how much my mother had told me about becoming a woman? So there I was upon arrival, Miss Pretty Future Scholarship Girl, mortified, asking a skinny adolescent male in the Hudson's Bay Company Post for a belt and pads, suffering the everyday indignities like everyone else who lived in, and had to slog through, that Slough of Despond.

"May I have a belt and pads for my period, please?" I was terrified he was going to ask me what size next.

"Ma'am, let me check." Of course, the girls who laughed at me were now standing beside me buying candy...

What I did not notice at the time was his professionalism, his kindness, and his discretion with the bag and its contents. However, I still had to carry the bag and its contents around with me for what seemed hours. Finally, in the school washroom, I tried to put it on. The pads were huge, uncomfortable, built for Amazons, and obviously designed by a male engineer. One of his ancestors had to have designed iron chastity belts.

Prison may be a better pastime than staying in Moosonee. Founded as recently as 1893 by the Revillon Brothers, competitors of the Hudson's Bay Company, Moosonee was a fur trading post that went bankrupt in 1936. I can see why. It is still bankrupt. A museum to this one interesting aspect of the place was shut. The population continues to sink. The only escape (besides the train) is to take the ferry to the (slightly) more successful outpost of Moose Factory, on an island of the Moose Flats, in the middle of the Moose

River. It has a nice old Church, which, when we were there, was full of respectful Cree who kindly welcomed us. I would talk more about Moose Factory, except that while we were standing on the dock waiting for the ferry to go back, all the girls seemed to be attacked by blood-sucking leeches at the same time. As we learned, it is not so easy to remove them, and as we were all carrying our coats, we kept finding more of them until the next day! They are awful memories.

Well, my fading memory of the place maybe like those of others who have moved away to a better life elsewhere. Even at the time, it was clear to me that people have to have something to do; giving them a monthly cheque isn't enough. Little did I know then how its emptiness would echo my life's failures and disappointments. I just have not lived up to my promise, my potential, or my own ambitions. I denigrate Moosonee; I should talk about myself the same way.

Of course, we were supposed to enjoy our trip to Moosonee and write suitable glowing reports upon our return. My essay, "Stone Age Life – Then and Now," was not a glowing endorsement of the place and was, perhaps, unusual for a twelve-year-old. I do wonder what my teachers thought. Maybe they agreed with me and could not admit it. But come on, could there have been a bigger contrast between what we expected and what we experienced and between Moosonee, Ontario, and Washington, D.C.?

The Gathering Storm, 148 BC

The train ride back to Ottawa was even more unbearable. I decided it was time to be back with Cleopatra Thea (daydreams being very flexible as to historical accuracy, timing, and place), and it was dinner time in the palace. We were seated at long tables in the megaron (the major courtyard of the palace), and the heat of the day was only just beginning to fade. As Queen, I had the shade of a Morus tree. First came dancers wearing chitons (a draped and folded dress), stringing a barbiton lyre against their left hips, strummed by the right hand holding a plectrum (a tortoiseshell tool to pluck the strings) as they performed their dancing pose. Others followed, playing the aulos, the reed pipe, with the same slow and graceful motion of the dance. It was a fusion of dance and song. A little bird perched on the finger of the outstretched arm of the chorus leader, seemingly bewitched by his singing, as the chorus entered with prayers for the gods. The hetairai, the cultured and educated courtesans, in long lines like ants brought bowls of food to tables underneath the arches and columns.

Thaïs, my young and favourite maidservant, brought a kylix cup of wine to my lips with her unconsciously coquettish, endearingly childish, and innocent smile. She looked up at me; I dearly loved her, and she knew it and would do anything for me.

The food was divine, a mixture of salty, spicy and sweet flavours. Warm poppy seed bread; cheeses of goats, sheep, and camels; white, green, veined; soft and hard. Honey, olives, whipped egg and barley, meat with pickled and tangy peppers, yoghurts as thick as clotted cream, and finishing with nuts and figs! Fresh, ripe, welcoming figs! You open them with your fingers, revealing an unexpected world within.

Suddenly a messenger was brought in, followed by two naked, chained Saka warriors flanked by guards. A commotion erupted; conversations ceased. The Prytany, the leader of the boule or council, wise old Tyndaeus, the last direct descendant from Alexander's Companions, rose from his seat and addressed the King, my brother:

"My King, we cannot have these naked savages brought before us on such a feast day…"

Antiochus rose from his seat, raising his hand to stop Tyndaeus. "I, Antiochus, your King, demand your attention. Did not Alexander marry a Sogdian? Our priests have read the livers and have said we are to learn from the Saka."

Tyndaeus replied, shaking his head, "But these are not Greek priests; they are Assyrians who flay their prisoners and children alive; who impale and blind their vassals…"

I thought to myself, as I looked out of the window to the electrum-covered statue of Jupiter below, what indeed were Greeks doing so far from home in an alien land with a different history, different customs, and different languages? It seemed obvious to me that my brother was misreading the coming apocalypse. Times were bad and getting worse.

"Silence, we will hear the messenger."

The messenger began, "We great you, Antiochus, King of Kings, we Saka come in peace, and seek only lands to farm and raise our families, for we flee the Yuezhi who have stolen our lands and livestock from the great steppes beyond the mountains. We only fight when your soldiers attack us; we have no choice."

Tyndaeus continued, "My Lord, they have better bows, they kill from horseback, they rob and burn our farms and burn our gods….the storm is about to break upon us!"

"Remove him," and soldiers led him, gesticulating and complaining, away.

"Brother, should you not listen to the council of the wise?" I turned to my husband, who was red in the face.

"Queen, we have experts who know these things; we are few, and they are many. We will rely on the priests' reading of the omens. You will please and soften me now in my chambers; bring your pretty cupbearer, too".

Rites of Passage, 1975

Away from home! No, my mother and father did not come with me to see me settled in at Annesley Hall at Victoria College. I had chosen Victoria College as they offered me two scholarships, and other schools had only offered me one. Now for more on the scholarship story. Two scholarships meant that I would make money going to school and would not have to ask my parents for money! Unfortunately, this debacle was to teach me another lesson. After I arrived, I only received one scholarship from the Bursar's Office. No explanation was offered. I went to the Registrar's Office to inquire where the second cheque was. I showed them the two different letters naming two different scholarships on official letterheads, one from the University of Toronto and one from Victoria College. The Gorgons behind the barriers in the office would not give me my second cheque and would not say why. I asked to see the Registrar, the Dean, or the Bursar, or all of them if they would not talk to me. They said they were too busy – and the office was closing for the day at ten minutes to twelve. I said the sign on the door said the office was open until noon…you can sense where this is going. So I left a note for any of them to call me. After vainly waiting for two more weeks, I returned, and they again demanded to know why I wanted to see them. I told them it was obvious why I wanted to see them if I had two letters naming two different scholarships, and they had only given me one. They would not give me an appointment. So, I raised my voice in the office until

I got to see the Dean and the Bursar. When I did, instead of apologizing, the Bursar said:

"You only get one scholarship." He could not bring himself to say, "Sorry, we made a mistake." Worse, he told me to sit down while he towered over me and asked for help from the Dean as he was frightened of a 16-year-old. I remember looking up at the ugly, red, pus-oozing eruption on his chin. He tried to make it look as though it was MY fault that I had been sent two scholarship letters by Victoria College and the University of Toronto. How dare I ask what the two letters said I should get? I thus learned the game Stalin used so well. Make them fearful, intimidate them, and make them cry. The powerful love to hurt the less powerful. It is always about control. A young girl of 16 is an easy victim. The Dean was almost as bad. They enjoyed it. I will never forget those bastards. After graduating, I have never given Victoria College a penny. And never will. A certain type of person enjoys being cruel. Kindness is a gift to be treasured and rare amongst little men promoted above their competence. And apologizing is not possible for someone who has no sense of decency.

When I was there, Northrop Frye was still alive and lecturing. You would often see him – somewhat shorter in stature than you might have otherwise thought from all the accolades – walking across the quadrangle to the library. Nowadays, I see there is a bronze stature to him outside the E.J. Pratt Library, (we thought it clever to change the name and add the P of Pratt to the initials, making it the E.J.P. Rat library. Small things please small minds, they say). Back then, there was a picture of him sitting without a chair, floating as it were, in the air, amongst clouds, over the Reading Room tables. They thought he was a god. I did, too, until I heard him read the opening lines of Paradise Lost. Someone asked him to start the annual opening public lecture for the reading of the blind man Milton's great poem.

So, we are seated in the grand auditorium, with the self-important professors smugly thinking how clever they were, all lined up at the back of the New Academic Building, waiting for the rousing lines of "Of Mans First Disobedience and the Fruit/Of that Forbidden Tree, whose mortal taste/Brought Death into the World, and all our woe…" and, well, he begins, and he can't read. It would be like asking me to pitch the opening ball for the World Series. I can't throw a ball. His mutilation of the language was what I would do to the ball…. most likely, what I threw would roll along the ground for five feet, where it would stop and look forlorn. His reading was worse than butchering; it was pathetic. He stumbled over the words and then read with the inflection of a robot. His reading was on par with having to listen to tax accountants discuss deferring taxes on bond discounts of inter-company bonds as they are amortized – when you would rather go out to play with your Barbies. It certainly was not the enthroned All-Powerful God kicking Lucifer out of heaven, shrinking him to the size of a pea! I got up and walked out. The professors glared that I had such audacity.

One of Frye's specialties was William Blake, and he came to our Romantic Poetry class to speak about Blake's illustrated book "America, a Prophecy." I had already made up my mind about Northrop Frye before he opened his mouth – first impressions count. Michael, a large Oshawa lad who worked on the GM lines in the summer (I liked him too, but he had too many zits), started to question everything Frye said. When Frye said Blake meant 'x,' Michael would interrupt and say "Why couldn't it be 'z'?" Every time this happened, Frye agreed and said it could indeed be 'z.' At the time, I laughed and thought less of Frye and that this was all a waste of time. How could truth have such diametrically opposite meanings?

Since that day, however, my opinion of Blake's "glorious luminosity" and Northrop Frye's perspicacity and insights have grown immeasurably. Since then, too, Michael came out gay and died a sad and broken drunk. Northrop's life had been good; what had gone so wrong with Michael's? What was it Mark Twain said, 'It was amazing how much my father learned in the two years I was away at college?' Maybe, indeed, Northrop Frye had not been able to read Milton well if he had been suffering from incipient dementia or something else…. who knows the real story?

***

But back on that arrival day in September, I had to get a taxi and a porter to help me with my steamer trunk from the bus station. It was heavy. All the less fortunate people in life take the bus. At least, this is the case in Canada. Over the ensuing years, I would get to know these poorer people well. They were nicer than the rich Rosedale people, more accepting of people that are different and flawed. The rich, if they admit to their own flaws, will be even less accepting of those with their own flaws. Arriving at Annesley Hall, other girls had parents with them. They helped get them settled. I had another reason to dislike my parents. I was alone.

Coming of Age, 1975

The girls were nice to me. Over the next few months – and years – they told me about how to look after my hair, eyebrows, lipstick, how to shave lower legs, armpit hair, deodorant, washing more often, and even using tampons. They had rather made fun of my belts. Some did not wear panties under their PJs. My roommate, Ann, was making love to her boyfriend and living at his place most of the time. I seldom saw her. Her parents had no idea. I wanted to belong and to be like the others. I quickly learned how other people had led very different lives. It intrigued me, and I wanted to learn about these other lives. I wanted to live a different life and pretend to be someone I was not. I wanted to belong, to not look and act differently than they did. I didn't want to stand out anymore. It was a mistake.

Some girls with smaller breasts didn't wear a bra, and you could see their nipples. This rather turned me on. Valerie would daringly unbutton her blouse a few buttons more than I would have dared. The men loved it. They could look down her blouse and, if lucky, see a nipple. A small nipple. I couldn't do that, as my bosom was large. And my nipples didn't seem to get as hard as hers did. I liked thinking about her nipples. The Vic Pub was Thursday night and Friday night. Wow! That was fun! One girl who was in geology was also a ballet dancer; she taught me how to stand and walk and sit demurely – and rather sexually, too. It all helped. They were nice. Normal girls who genuinely wanted to help. I was 16. I felt out of it.

A nerd. Not one of them. And being nearly three years younger than most of the girls was too big a gap.

There was the Toronto Youth Orchestra; they accepted me after a short audition. I liked that. I liked walking over to the Royal Conservatory along Bloor St. I felt so grown up and that I had arrived. There was a notice posted on the board asking for people that could coach students. I was no teacher, but I helped some at the Royal Conservatory with courses on such arcane subjects as counterpoint. Some of my students were more than twice my age. I didn't find these things difficult; I just thought it neat how music could be both harmonically interdependent and yet melodically independent. School came easily to me; I just wish life had, too. Or maybe a better way of saying that is that because school came so easily to me, I thought life would, too.

But more importantly, I had discovered another side of boys. And passion. The more I had, the more I liked – and wanted. Men. Men were my downfall. In high school, I had crushes on boys, but there was no sex, and it was all so dreamlike and unreal. I had been oblivious to making love. I was rather innocent. Of course, today, we have feminism, and maybe girls grow up even sooner. Of course, all men are bad anyway. But the problem is we need them, at least sometimes. Or at least I do. Men only want one thing; they want it all the time, and, more or less, they are all the same. It just seemed so physical to them. But I don't blame the lion for wanting his pride or to protect his pride. I rather like the lion! Or to be a lion myself.

We can't run away from nature. I thought I had been living in a cloud somewhere. Let me tell you, I enjoyed sex.

***

Hendrik the Hermit, I called him, although he was not. Hendrik was from Kingsville, a small village somewhere in southern Ontario that had never been heard of by anyone, anywhere. He didn't care if you liked him or not. His Dad was a farmer, and he wanted to be a farmer. Hendrik had a mischievous bent and lived in – yes, you guessed it – South House. I had already caught him red-handed in a number of his minor exploits like panty raids. In those far-off days, there was a men's residence and a ladies' residence. Girls came to the men's residence, Burwash Hall, for food on Saturdays, and the boys came to the girls', Annesley Hall, on Sundays.

One such Saturday, I was behind him in the line at Burwash Hall to get our cafeteria-style food (one slice of meat, one potato, waterlogged and overcooked veggies, two pieces of bread, one glass of chocolate milk, etc. – prison food was indeed better). I saw him push human teeth into the self-serve row of bran and blueberry muffins. He was in front of me in line (I had pushed my way forward to be near him). I did think it, as awful as it sounds, very funny. The next ten minutes would be pure anticipatory excitement, waiting to see who would scream first. He was clearly nervous, but he always seemed to get all the luck. The most prim and proper girl, Jennifer, a thin and bespectacled girl in a white blouse from Beamsville, Ontario (a place famous for inventing the ice hockey net) – who always went to Church on Sunday mornings – picked the spiked muffin with a human tooth. The screams were indeed memorable, the disruption immense. Wooden chairs were pushed back hurriedly and noisily; some of them fell over backwards as people stood up, creating a cacophony. Quickly, people came rushing over to see how and what had happened. Burwash Hall was notorious for its echoes! Hendrik was as shocked as everyone else. I confronted him afterwards, and he smiled from ear to ear. I don't think I have ever seen such a big smile before or since on anyone. They never caught him.

His next prank was classic. I had to make sure girls picked the planted trap; for maximum effect, you had to make sure there was a gaggle of girls in the line after the plant was set and the trap sprung. Hendrik was taking "pre-med" – that compulsory group of courses many students took in the vain attempt to get into 'med school,' the ticket to wealth and recognition. Most, like Hendrik, failed to get the needed grades. In his case, he wanted to fail so that he could say to his parents that he didn't have the right stuff to be a doctor. But as he was enrolled in the correct courses, he was able to get the samples he needed for his next rather nasty trick. Hendrik got fertilized eggs from the Med. Sci. Building's laboratories and cooked them slowly and carefully in the basement kitchen of his residence. Then he brought them, still warm, and put them in the "five-minute soft egg" row of eggs at Burwash Hall. You wanted the eggs opened to be eaten in Burwash Hall for two reasons. One, the "hard-boiled eggs" row of eggs might be eaten later – and that would spoil the effect if they were opened in a small gathering elsewhere, say, in a study session of a "Women Are People" focus group and the second reason was that screams echoed so much better in Burwash Hall. Burwash Hall had this high, high ceiling. It really was a lovely building in the English style of mediaeval dining halls. It even had a High Table where the professors sat. Above the High Table was framed the flag that had covered Queen Victoria's, the Empress of India's, coffin at her funeral. It was grand. And no location would serve better the discovery of a cooked, dead baby chick on your breakfast plate. Let me tell you, you never forget the screams and commotion – especially when the second and third such chicks were found. I must say I do feel sorry for the poor supplier of eggs, who claimed he had no roosters…

Hendrik was trouble – but he did not want a girlfriend. There were steam tunnels under the men's residences and under the girls', and you could easily travel underground using them to get to the respective kitchens. He and his friends stole meat from the women's kitchens' freezers, and I even watched while he masturbated into the vat of porridge that was kept there. I stopped eating porridge. His residence made beer there, too, which tasted horrid. They kept adding sugar to the beer to raise the alcoholic content so that not only did the concoction taste more like syrup than beer but, more dangerously, the bottles could spontaneously explode from the higher pressure. But all good times come to an end. The year I left Victoria College, all the residents of South House were kicked out.

And if you were thinking I had more to do with the teeth and chickens story than I am letting on, you're right.

I was developing a nastier side of my character. I think it started as a child when I organized the boys of the street to be naughty by ringing doorbells and running away…I found it easy to get people to do naughty things without me having to do anything except suggest it. Thus, I found I could get what I wanted with even less effort.

The world is divided into Givers and Takers, and I was learning to be a Taker and to surround myself with Givers. It was not a good thing. I confused giving, or generosity, with timidity rather than empathy.

Exiting the Nietzschean Cave, 1977

I loved the violin. Verlaine described '*Les sanglots longs/des violons/de l'automne*' – the long sobs of violins in the autumn. I can't speak French, but these sad words seem to drag themselves along like the melancholy of autumn itself. Well, it was autumn when I met him. Yevgeny Volkov. The Noble Wolf. Nothing matches the passion, the pain, the suffering, the ecstasy, the soaring, and the diving, that relaxing release of the violin's music. It just carries you away. And how he played the violin! Then I remembered that day he had asked me to play Thaïs. The music is nostalgic, hopeful, tender – and yet dangerously poignant, sentimental, and unresolved. As I played, I saw his eyes were wet. Me! I had made his eyes wet! I was his forever. Like Nietzsche's Zarathustra, I had come out of the cave from the gloomy mountains of my upbringing and found sunshine and sunlight looking upon the Noble Wolf! My time had come! Or so it seemed at the time…

I had first seen him at the Royal Conservatory. Then at a party. Some drip had walked up and given me a Singapore Sling and was then trying to get my 'phone number, and then I saw him arrive.

"Next!" I said dismissively to my admirer and turning away; I caught Yevgeny's eye. He walked over to me, and I started to melt. "I heard you play today," I managed.

"I know you play well…" he said with a strong Russian accent, dragging out the syllables and words as they do "…Yelena."

He even knew my name! Wow! And he said 'Helen' like Yelena, with that "l" spoken at the back of the throat. It was magical to me. West-end Ottawa was not for me anymore.

Other women noticed me with him. I liked that. I liked how other women were jealous. I liked being the centre of attention. He was a lot older than me. He was a violinist in a real orchestra, not some youth orchestra filled with rich kids that wanted to be noticed. All women were after him, and he had walked up to me. He liked *me.* He had passion; he was alive. And I was young.

He smoked like a chimney. He smoked Gitanes. He was cool. His head was crowned with wild hair in all directions. His smile was electric; he had presence off the stage, and, wow, on the stage, you just drooled. In his performance, the clothes on his chest expanded beneath his white shirt, and I just wanted him. He invited me to his next performance at Massey Hall (Roy Thomson Hall didn't open until 1982). Yes, this was all a long time ago, dear readers.

I went to him, behind the stage, in his dressing room. The ushers waved me through. Being pretty has its own privilege. I was wearing long white pants, high heels, with long hair. He was sitting, smoking. I wanted to smoke. I wanted to be Lauren Bacall, long, slinky, sexy with dirty blonde hair and a deep smoky voice. Walking in on him, then, I think he thought I was. I went to him, saying nothing. It was a start of a whirlwind romance.

He was uncircumcised and clearly never washed under his foreskin. His cock stank.

I had loved Dr. Zhivago. It was my favourite film growing up. The music was a grand sweep, the opening of the film, the coffin, and the burial. That scene of the procession! The branch rattled on the window at night. The horror of looking at his dead mother in the coffin. The little boy, all alone in that bleak wilderness. (Had I wished my mother was in that coffin?) Of course, I would remember the lovelorn Strelnikov, the revolutionary of the film who loses his reason and the love of his life over a mad infatuation with Bolshevism. He lost his sense of proportion, the central purpose of life and his grounding in reality in a headlong dash to utopian ideology. Worse, he seems to relish his and seek his own downfall. My, oh my. Who else would do that?

In the film, Dr. Zhivago sleeps with his mistress in the ice-covered dacha. It does look as though they are having fun. When I first saw the film, I asked my mother why she was sleeping with someone who was not her husband (what an insufferably inquisitive child I must have been), and she said it was because it was cold. At that age, it seemed it would be fun to be a mistress and a kept woman. Even my mother did it, I thought. You can see where this is going.

But Yevgeny, to me, was more than a film reborn in life. His grandparents had escaped the Russian Revolution. They had been White Russians. They had been valiant; fought for a lost cause,

Tsarist Russia. The Bolshevik miasma had carried off a way of life and the total collapse of an entire civilization. They fled to the Crimea with General Kolchak; that noble General who was to die for his cause. Yevgeny's grandfather had fought his way to Ekaterinburg in a vain attempt to rescue the Tsar. They had arrived only days too late. This history was noble. It was Hector at Troy all over again. It was exotic and far away. It was valiant. It was a Lost Cause, and the white expanse of Siberian winter covered the grandparents' retreat to Vladivostok, then to Shanghai, California, and then to Canada. The grand sweep of the world was too much for me. Wow. And then he had wanted to marry me.

He told me I had great talent, that my playing would carry me to a great orchestra.

Then why did he have a girlfriend like Polina? She was as plain as she was boring. Quiet, well-behaved. I called her the "homely hippie" for the long, slightly Bohemian look of her clothes. She was hardly pretty. She worshipped him as a devotee at the altar of the Great Yevgeny…well, how else could I describe her? She was a sycophant, a brainless slave. I didn't like her.

"Can you come to a party I am having for Yevi, Helen?" she asked. "It's next Saturday, after the rehearsal. I go to all of his rehearsals." (She had that irritating Boston accent where vowels become nasal and the sentences end in an up note rather than the more typical down note).

Yevi? You call him Yevi? What a stupid diminutive! I was pissed.

"I'm making a quilt for Yevi, and I thought you might like to help, too," she smiled. "I know you like him." She gave me a knowing look and a light nudge. Oh yes, I am going to sit around with you, eat cookies and drink milk, bitch. I really want to help you steal him away from me, too. God, what did he see in her? She had these small pointy breasts – which would sag horribly – and shapeless pencil legs. She couldn't be bright in school.

"What do you take at school, Polina?" I innocently asked....

"Oh, I don't go to school. It's a full-time job looking after Yevi." I probably scowled. "I do like your shirt, Helen."

I was wearing a Maple Leafs jersey that Paul had just given me. Yes, I had another boyfriend too, Paul Emerson. I was going to Christmas concerts with Yevgeny behind Paul's back. At the same time, I was fucking Paul in the stacks at Robarts library. Yevgeny sent flowers to me every time we made love. Well, I bet Polina wasn't getting flowers.

I was still young. And it was fun to have sex with two different men. The fear of a black swan event – being caught with both or the other – was intoxicating. I had some growing up to do. C.S. Lewis says virtue is creative and fascinating as it is so rare, but I rather liked the excitement and pleasure of sin.

It was a brand-new jersey, and I knew it was expensive. I was trying to conform, to be a normal girlfriend, and to be the archetypal all-Canadian Leaf fan myself…Paul loved it when I wore nothing under it, and he slipped his hands up there. I could feel his hands tremble.

"Thanks, Polina, I'd love to come. Can I bring anything?" I could pretend to care.

"Oh, just your sweet self!" Ya, right, bitch. The homely hippie. I give Yevgeny what he wants, I thought. I'll show you. She had this tie-dyed blouse on that made her look ten years out of date and had this ugly, frizzled, dyed blonde hair. Her hair was awful. I'll show you. How could anyone like that hair? It made her look ten years older than she must have been…

Part II

La Mancornadora

(The Unfaithful One)

Like the two currents passing each other at Byzantium, the deep cold from the Black Sea, and the warm surface from the Aegean, lovers can misunderstand, miscalculate or – as in my case – betray. The pain scars the hearts of the loved ones – often with the damage done unknown. Oh, if I could have avoided the suffering I caused from the farewells of my mistakes!

Falling Off the Edge of the Slippery Slope, 1981

Years seem to pass. I did not go home to Ottawa anymore. I went to Law School.

"Helen, is that you?" I swung around.

"Christiaan! What are you doing here?"

"Walking down Bloor St!"

I had not seen Christiaan in years. "I mean, what are you doing *here*?"

"Repairing clocks. You know, the old ones that chime and sit on the mantelpiece that no one keeps anymore." He told me he had quit university and, not knowing what to do, had moved to Toronto. We decided to grab a bite at the Swiss Chalet – a restaurant that was neither Swiss nor a chalet – on Bloor St. It was practically across the street from the Royal Conservatory.

Christiaan had lived near me in Ottawa and had had, in younger days, I knew, a crush on me. He would follow me home, always a distance behind, but was too shy to approach. I did know he always watched me – and I thought him a harmless, wimpy nerd. He didn't struggle in school, but he never excelled. He was nice, but a bit too boring - I thought. He had a few friends – mostly beta male types like him who seemed, most of the time, to be invisible. They were the types who did not wear flared jeans, etc., when everyone else did. They probably went home and read second-rate science fiction books, dreaming of things they were not and never could be.

But he was always "there," a touchstone and a connection to the past. I knew I could trust him.

"I lied a bit. I fix clocks, but that doesn't pay – but it sounds good. To pay the bills, I'm a manager at Jean Junction. Most of the time, I rearrange piles of jeans during the day and then spend the nights trying to reconcile the deposit of the day's takings. Problem is, I could never add." Christiaan explained as we organized the chairs. It was cold outside, and we had to take our coats off and arrange them on chairs in that peculiarly Canadian winter ritual. "It's a shit job, but it pays well enough, and it gives me time to fix clocks, too."

Clocks? I had a use for Christiaan. But I had to warm him up to it. "Do you remember me asking if you wore wooden shoes at home?"

"Oh yes, and I told you I wore them to bed." We smiled, and we continued our reminiscences. The waitress came and we ordered coffee.

So, dear reader, I started to tell him more of my life…we talked and talked. We did revisit the famous library scene. The library of Riverside High School was the best; it was a refuge. It had the complete Loeb Classical Library, and I wanted to read every volume from beginning to the end. Completing that task was yet another of my many failures. I got sidetracked reading Xenophon's

Oeconomicus, a book, on the surface, about the importance of the woman of the house running the complexity of the ancient Greek household with slaves, food preparation, cleaning, cooking, weaving, etc. Even in high school, I saw that it was an ironic book, actually making fun of misogynistic Ischomachus, and was a much more important book with criticisms of Athenian society and really about how the state should be run. Xenophon was a genius – a great general and strategist who both led the largest mercenary army to Persia and back again, and, as a philosopher who wrote the best Apology for Socrates after his trial and execution. Xenophon wrote about Ideals and the importance of self-control. Xenophon is sadly unrecognized today. How to be a *better* human being. Can you imagine how he would be received today? Michel Foucault is one of the philosophers you read about these days, but back then, in high school, I had not even heard of Michel Foucault. Michel Foucault was a French philosopher who delighted in violating social norms – from promoting unprotected sex to claiming young children could – and did – consent to sex with adults. He was an unpleasant and totally amoral man. And people read and listen to Foucault, rather than read the famous general of the ten thousand – and don't get the satire and irony of *Oeconomicus*? What does that tell you about the modern age? But I digress. The librarians were excellent; the library even subscribed to magazines like Encounter and The Economist. It also subscribed to Sports Illustrated, so that boys could have something to borrow in the bathroom to masturbate to when the swimsuit edition came out. I found then that boys do not know how to concentrate on serious issues.

Anyway, Christiaan would come and watch me read in the library. I didn't think he was creepy; he was too gentle and kind. He was just a nerd – and I was too busy.

It was Christiaan who brought up the library story. It was just before the final Grade 13 Biology exam, which was the easiest 100% I ever got in a course as it was only memory work. I was reading another textbook as I was trying to learn more about Kreb's Cycle. A group of "in girls" came in, and they started to make fun of the fact I was using the wrong textbook. (These were not the type of people who were to enjoy organic chemistry at the University of Toronto. Well, I have to brag about something here. I got an "A" in Chem. 230. So, you can understand why these girls (they weren't very pretty, either) really got under my skin).

Now, this old library of Riverside High was huge, stretching the full expanse of the front of the building, with a high ceiling. Gone now is that temple to excellence and learning. No longer are we proud to stand upon the shoulders of the Greats that went before us. Today, in the age of thirty-second sound bites, the library is a computer station with books banished; we all, apparently, now want to stand in a swamp to be bitten by midges, doing it "my way," ignorant of the past.

Back in my day, to cool the library (it did get hot in there), there was a monstrous fan on a stand behind the last table. The girls had gone to that one, where they proceeded to talk loudly. They started to share notes – presumably cheat sheets, as our teacher, Mrs. Agatha Harding (I called her ἀγᾰθή, "the good," her name in Greek), was too trusting and tended to leave the class during the exam. (I could never understand cheat sheets – by the time you found and checked the answer, you could have answered another question). Anyway, they spread their loose papers all over the table. They ignored everyone in the library, talking loudly, totally engrossed in themselves. I walked to the fan, pointed it down, and plugged it in.

The girls, being stupid and not understanding basic physics, started to chase the papers (which were now flying all over the library) and began rushing about, falling over each other – instead of just unplugging the fan. I walked out, expecting to get in trouble with the librarian, as she would have seen everything. Instead, the librarian took me aside, gave me a book, and said:

"Helen, I thought you might like this book. It is about Dorothy Hodgkin, a girl who went to a school in a little town in England and yet went on to win the Nobel Prize in chemistry. Crystallography - I think it has to do with X-rays and crystallography." Of course, my shadow Christiaan had been in the library that day, just watching and listening intently.

***

Sitting opposite to me, it was clear he still worshipped me. It is nice to be liked.

"I have a job for you," I said, changing the subject. "It is quite a coincidence, but my boyfriend's father has a broken clock. The clock is from George II, 1740s, an Act of Parliament Clock or something like that. It is a real antique, and few know how to fix it. It is in the hall, high up on the wall, you'll need a ladder. Can you fix it?"

"I'd love to see the clock…You obviously have a boyfriend now…"

Um, I could not tell him how wild I had become. So, I would downplay the fun I had at university to him.

"Actually, I have two and don't know what to do. Paul's dad, though, is a piece of work.

You will need to get something in writing first of all – so you get paid for your work." Later, I arranged an appointment with Paul for him to come in two weeks' time.

The Lull Before the Storm, 1980

Paul Emerson had a Mazda RX-7. He was tall, good-looking, and played hockey; he was the all-Canadian kid. He liked me. He was in law school with me, and I first met him on the very first day of school when we fumbled together coming in the front door of Osgoode Hall together. Now, if that wasn't fate, what is?

I could be like everyone else. I wore the Toronto Maple Leafs jersey he gave me and started to go to games at the Gardens. I went to his practices for his team. I could be a normal Canadian girl, too. Yes, I was back eating hot dogs, though now at the hockey area food concessions with those bald fluorescent lights and hard, echoing halls with unpainted concrete floors. I was even squeezing ketchup and mustard from those annoying plastic pouches, usually onto everything except the dog itself. The arenas were always cold.

I knew he liked how I got into his car and how my dress would ride up as we drove around. (Guys like a bit of leg and cleavage). I helped him change gears; my parents had a manual transmission car, and I impressed Paul with how I could drive a manual. Forbidden to learn to drive our car by my mother, she had not known I had practiced brake-clutch-neutral to stop and neutral-clutch-gas to go for hours on the driveway when she was out. I could even turn the Pontiac (aka Vauxhall) Firenza around on the driveway.

"Saw the Leafs game?"

"No, I was reading about Byzantium."

"Who's he?" I don't think Paul had ever read a book for pleasure. He had a high, bare forehead, crowned with a thick crop of black hair with a lovely gentle wave in it. He had small eyes set deep below strong eyebrows and a straight, thin nose. His cheeks were large, flat, and incredibly soft – it seemed to be because his beard seemed to stop at his pale lips. When he didn't shave, the stubble petered out as it climbed above his cheeks. It was cute. When we went out, we looked a nice pair, me with bright red lipstick, globular earrings, and long hair, all tucked in under his armpit as we walked along together. He had a very boyish look and feel. He was tall.

They were wealthy beyond belief, and his dad's business acumen bred success after success. The family had no imagination and worshipped Mammon. It was all about money, and anything they touched turned to gold. His father did not know who Midas was. And starting first-year law at U. of T., his dad had already arranged an articling position for Paul at Tory Tory, a premier law firm.

They lived in Rosedale. They lived on Roxborough Drive, on a slight rise, in the most fabulously turreted Romanesque Revival-come-Queen Anne house Victorian Toronto ever produced. It exuded class, prestige, success, and deep-rooted "arrival." It had everything. An asymmetrical façade; multiple, pedimented porches on different levels; cantilevered Dutch gables; patterned shingles, tiles, and relief panels; oriel and bay windows; columns, pilasters, cone-shaped and complicated roofs and inspired Gothic stained and leaded, cut, and horizontal glass. I dreamed about who had lived there before the Emersons. Probably, it was built by a sober Presbyterian pastor at the turn of the century, who translated Biblical Hebrew at his desk in the turret before looking out over Rosedale Valley…I loved their house more than they did, or at least I thought about its details more than they did. What lovely memories I have of that house to this day. I can still see myself exploring the secrets, the corners, and the intricate details of master craftsmen.

I don't think the parents approved of me – but likely, they would not have approved of anyone from out of town and from a less privileged background than their own. I didn't even know what Lake Rosseau was all about. I was soon to learn. Oh yes, they had cedar strip canoes and wooden motorboats from the 1930s at the cottage.

They first time I met Paul's parents, his mother had just had a hysterectomy and was only just back from the hospital, and the father was making some deal on the phone. Paul Senior was in some type of real estate development-cum-construction business. Although they were not Jewish (many Toronto property developers are), I got the sense they were not the old money of the St. James Cathedral clique but more "nouveau riche." He was always talking about his "connexions" – it all sounded a tad shady to me. The mother was different. She was of a slight build, insecure, mild, but caring, and had no opinions other than her husband's. She assumed she was to come home from the hospital and to immediately cook me a fancy dinner, despite being weak and ill. She knew her place, and her family's place, in the cosmos. I liked her, as she was fragile. But there was also something missing. When I later learned that Paul's younger brother, John, had hanged himself on a tree in the park across the street, she had this vacant look on her face. Not a vacant stare of shock, horror, or pain, but rather as though she had just said, "you know, this is Canada. It snows in the winter." It was a strangely upsetting fatalism.

Where he hung himself was the site of the old Lieutenant Governor's house in Chorley Park. The Lieutenant Governor's house, "the best-looking mansion ever built in Canada" (see pictures below), had been torn down in 1959 as this was Toronto, aka "Hog Town." Toronto is a great home for people like the Emersons, who loathe history, aesthetics, and culture. So, there was some irony to the beautiful building being torn down to be replaced, momentarily at least, by a young man who had hung himself. The mother, Marie, found him in the morning. She told me she had walked across the street "with her coffee cup, and there he was." The grounds had been lovingly landscaped by Frances Heakes, the official architect, and fifty years on, many of the trees were at their grandest peak. It was autumn; the morning was cool before the sun warmed, and the sugar maples were turning red around the old oak, where John hung, his face contorted in extremis. I can just imagine Marie looking at her son, hanging on the tree, sipping her coffee.

Marie had another side. She saw that I had the Curse and saw the rolling bouts of cramps would make me buckle in pain. The mother had opioids. She gave me some for the Curse. It was the start of a problem for much of my life. The pills helped. I became a slave to pills. A slow and dangerous descent. Their whole medicine cabinet was full of them. Even then, the drug companies were no doubt rubbing their hands in glee.

They took me to the RCYC, the Royal Canadian Yacht Club. They had a 32' Etchells racing yacht and a 1936 Chris Craft Commander. I had never been on a racing boat, let alone a hand-made wooden cruiser from the golden age of Gatsby. (Of course, they had never heard of Gatsby!) I loved the subdued sound of its dual engines, the gentle but unmistakably powerful, dull rumble. Power was there, if you needed it, sir. There were burls on the cherry woodwork by the table. The whole interior was cherry. It was a masterpiece of handmade skill, love, and excellence.

The RCYC lodge on the island looks back to Toronto. It is a gorgeous, white, two-story building with a balcony and verandah running around it on both levels. Ceiling fans slowly revolve around your head in the dining rooms, completing the image of a far-off colonial outpost of Her Majesty. One sunset, looking out to Toronto over the green lawn as its lights came on, I quipped, "I bet you can hear the temple bells a-callin', the flying fish play, as the sun comes up like thunder, 'crost the bay." Mrs. Emerson replied, helpfully pointing with her arm, "Actually, the sun comes up over there, in the east." No, she didn't know Kipling and hadn't been further than Florida. Well, I had never been anywhere either, but I could, and did, read…did she?

But I need to tell you two stories; it is funny how some stick in your memory. Sadly, or luckily, perhaps, I may have forgotten worse. I had just arrived, was walking alone along the quay, admiring all the lovely boats, wishing I had one, and walked past a particularly nice one with two women who were staring at me. One called out to me – rather rudely and imperiously, I thought, as they sipped on their drinks. They were in their tennis whites, fit, trim, and starting to wrinkle, but still annoyingly pretty, with that formulaic and identical, short, dyed, boring "no maintenance" hair required for Canadian women over 55. To me, that hair signals 'Husband, I am now an independent woman, 55+, and I am now identical to all of my sisters across Canada, and there is to be no more sex. We will all look the same and act as one. We will be a collective singular ME now.' The older, bossier one called out, "Who are you with? Are you one of the Curries' nieces?"

Sensing I was a bit put out, the other one stood up and said, "Hi, I'm Naomi Carey, and this is Sandra Thompson."

Sandra stood up and stretched her hand out, "I head the New Members Club, and we like to know all about them. Is this your first time here? I saw you came with the Emersons?"

"It is such a glorious day!" I replied.

'But what do you do?" I saw Paul coming, and I was about to say, "Oh, I do Paul; I'm an escort," but I held my tongue and said instead, turning as Paul came up, "Paul, you call me princess, don't you?"

Paul, ever obliging and totally smitten, replied on cue. "Of course, princess," allowing me to continue, "Oh, I don't DO anything, I am the granddaughter of the King of Albania, and we have a boat just like this to take us out to our cutter on the Adriatic." Their faces fell. "We do find you need a larger ship to go to Santorini. Nice to meet you." I shook their hands and left with Paul.

"How can you do that? I mean, we are members here, and they know everyone." Paul sounded more in awe than in anger. I am sure his mother got an earful.

As I love mornings (the light is always so even, the air clear and fresh, the smells so earthy), Paul and Paul Senior decided to take me sailing. I had never been sailing. Marie didn't sail, preferring only the motorboat. I was all a-quiver in anticipation. We were going to be part of some club race, and I had never been in a race either. I read all I could about racing and sailing – now I wanted to sail solo around the world, to run the Horn in late October, a prey hunted by a black storm, chasing me like a winged predator; to follow an albatross as it drifts across the sky, to see the wicked phosphorescence of the sea at night; to feel your tongue as dry as ashes as the shrunken boards curl under the sun, the boat becalmed on a painted ocean, with not a drop to drink for the mariner.

We arrived early. We had had breakfast. I had eaten fried eggs, hash browns, and bacon. I also drank two tall glasses of champagne and orange juice. Then we out onto the lake, past the airport breakwaters, and soon were listening only to 'the wind's song and the white sail's shaking'…the flying clouds, the flung spray and crying gulls…

The spinnaker was raised; it filled, and on the edge of the roaring wind, we raced, the horizon and shore rising and falling. Then I puked.

The worst thing about puking is not the actual puking. It is cleaning up the puke afterwards. The smell makes me dizzy and retch. Always concerned about appearances (haha), I kept my head down and hoped Sandra and Naomi could not smell it as they walked past the boat back to the clubhouse. I did think (being of famous royal lineage myself, of course – remember Queen Thea) that even Her Majesty the Queen makes smells when she has to go to the toilet.

The RCYC has two ferries, originally steamboats, the Hiawatha and the Kwasind, and they are the oldest active boats on Llyod's Registry. For over a hundred years, they have carried members and their guests to and from the island. They are elegant boats with long, flowing lines gently curving along the beam. Both are gracious old boats, but the Hiawatha infinitely more so. If you go to the ferry terminal, you will see her, quietly moored by her separate pier, silent testimony to a time that is past, pressed only into service when required by demand. Stalwart, loyal, faithful; a reflection of an ideal world long gone…

The Swing of Fortune's Wheel, 1981

And then it happened all so quickly. It was all a daze then, and now, all these years later, it seems to have happened on the same day. It was all within two weeks, as that was the date when I had met Christiaan at the Swiss chalet and when he was to go to the Roxborough house.

I had never liked the way the father, Paul Senior, was always standing so close to me, touching me unnecessarily, or how he would try to find me alone. At that time, I had just wanted to conform, to be liked, to be accepted, and to be less of a nerd. But I did not want to be around an old man trying to paw me. I had told Paul how uncomfortable I was around him, but he dismissed my concerns. "Naw, he means nothing," he would say. I then raised it with Paul Senior, asking for more room, saying how uncomfortable I was, and he said, "I'm a man; it's normal." I didn't think that there was any point in talking to Marie.

And then the day came when Marie saw him grab and try to kiss me; she saw me throw a frightened look at her, and yet she said nothing. On the way out that night, she gave me a large bottle of pills for the Curse. Maybe that was why she was slim.

It seems now that it was the very next day Paul announced, "Let's go to Las Vegas for the honeymoon."

"But we are not even engaged, Paul, and we are still in school." I was surprised. "And besides," I continued, "I am not going to Las Vegas for a honeymoon. Everything is fake in Las Vegas. Might as well get married to Mickey Mouse in Disneyland!"

"Ok, how about Disneyland?" Paul hopefully proffered. Disneyland was even worse, the epitome of maudlin, commercialized, fake America.

Desperate, I said, "How about Hawaii?" At least that had the sea and mountains…. The next day, I knew he had been at the Eaton Centre. He must have stopped at Birk's Jewellery. He announced our engagement at dinner when he gave it to me. He hadn't even asked me. I was shocked. I didn't know what to do. It was a ring with a giant rock. Now I was panicking.

Suddenly, wedding plans were advancing by themselves, like a tumbril bouncing unevenly and roughly over the cobbles to the guillotine. I had read about Las Vegas. The one big wide street, filled with blinking lights, beautiful people; sad, blank-faced, crazed gamblers; hookers looking for a trick and absurd games whose sole aim is to take your money with psychological hypnotism and statistical odds. Pathetic. One street over, the lights were poor, the giant garbage bins were on wheels, and the sad and homeless people lived and begged. It really was a whited sepulchre.

I was not going to Las Vegas. In my imagination, I seemed to hear shouting from the crowds standing at the side of the road. Were they egging the tumbril on for my execution? Or shouting for me to get off?

Now there was talk of 500 guests, ten types of champagne, Ossetian caviar, tents for guests' dogs and attendants for their horses, and on and on. Well, I exaggerate, but not by much. I forgot to mention the reception was to be at their farm in the rolling hills northwest of Toronto. That's the thing amongst the rich of Toronto – besides a nice house in Rosedale or Forest Hill and the obligatory cottage on a secluded lake, you also had a farm northwest of the city. God, that farm was another palace. All I could think of was Sassanid Persian Emperors, with palaces and pleasure gardens dotted all over their empire. I was just a marauding Xenophon, in awe, out of my depth, and overwhelmed with fine things that I had never seen before, arriving unexpectedly as a conquering hero at one of these palaces…I didn't belong here. And, anyway, the Sassanids were Zoroastrians – they exposed their dead to be eaten by vultures in a Dokhma, the silent tower of the dead – they didn't try and pretend that death was absent from their culture as we do now. Those ancient Persians not only understood the cycle of life and death, but they also had a greater appreciation of culture and art.

Paul was oblivious to my uncertainty. After dinner, we sat in their maple-panelled TV room, watching some sport of over-paid athletes on their huge television, a giant TV screen that did not give a focused picture. Giant TVs were crap in those days. Only someone with too much money and no idea of aesthetics would have bought one. People bought these things for bragging rights – I have money, look at me! They had three big red, green, and blue lights, which projected the picture and took up even more space behind the sofa. Then he wanted to make love to me. It was my fault as I had given him a copy of the Kama Sutra and had told him we had to try all the positions. You should have seen his eyes light up in amazement. It does not take much to please a man. I took more pills. Though it made the sex better, I was tired of a man crushing me – men just go on and on, thinking to themselves how good they are at sex. And we just want them to hurry up, finish their business, and get off us.

More to the point, I had another boyfriend and was not ready for marriage.

All I had been able to say at the dinner table, inexplicably, was, "Why do the Leafs always lose? Despite all their money, talk, support, fans, and media coverage, the Leafs always manage to lose." And to Torontonians, this pre-ordained fate of the Leafs losing is a perpetual surprise – even though the last time they won the Stanley Cup was 1967. It is as though Torontonians are surprised to see the sun set every evening. Oh, we thought the sun would stay up in the sky all night (No, you have to go north of Moosonee for that! Hahaha!), and the Leafs would go on to win ten to zip against Boston in the next game…(Oh, by the way, did I tell you Polina was from Boston and had that annoying accent, too? I did hate Boston, just like most Torontonians). Anyway, expressing doubts about the Leafs winning a game was tantamount to killing babies. I considered telling them I was a Habs fan (that has-been team from Montreal dismissed by Torontonians) just to annoy them. And thought better of it.

I really was not coping. I went home. On the telephone answering machine was a message from school asking me to come to see the Dean about my attendance and my exam results. And another one looking for rent. I had always excelled, and now I was failing. Things were going from bad to worse. It was true, I had not been to class and I had skipped exams. And I had not paid the rent. Oh, I could take the supplementals. I went to Yevgeny's and told him nothing.

The next morning, I walked over to Roxborough. I had a key, and no one would be home. I needed to talk to Paul and couldn't wait for him to come home. The walk would do me good.

As soon as I walked in the door (I had come in through the garage entrance to avoid nosy neighbours), I realised Paul Senior was home, and we surprised each other in the hall. The house had a grand hall.

"We need to talk," he began. "Now that you will be part of the family, you need to know my plan. You are really smart. I need that. You've got street smarts. My companies need that. One day, you will have all of this. Paul is too stupid to run the business. Nice kid, but really a leftie. Problem with lefties is that they never think for themselves. Every month is something new for them: hugging trees, promoting women, whatever. Can't run a business like that. I don't need a do-gooder giving needles to losers in a park. You've got the brains to run the show."

"I am not sure I know anything about business, Mr. Emerson. I am not sure I am the one for this."

"Oh, you are. But we need to make a deal. A secret deal. A man needs a woman from time to time, and girls like you need men, too. I understand that. Men are like women; women like men. You get my meaning?"

"No, I am sorry, I don't."

"You're hot. Really hot. I want to have sex with you from time to time. I know how to be discreet. We can fly to New York, hit some clubs, you'll like it. It'll be another life within a life. You're an *artiste*; it'll be great; you'll write poems!"

I found him repulsive. "I am sorry, but I am never going to have sex with you, Mr. Emerson."

"Helen, come on, you're no virgin. One day you will have all of this. Paul can't run the business. You've got the brains to run the show. The whole show. You'll get it all, and you and I can have a little secret and some fun. Paul doesn't even know what fun is."

"No, please, Mr. Emerson, this is not going to work."

"I know about Yevgeny; I know he's just a fling. It's OK, I understand. No one's home and I am a good lover. It's just you and me."

"What about Yevgeny?"

"I had you followed; it's OK. I like girls with spunk. You've got good spunk. You need sex, too, just like a man. Wish my kid had the balls you have. We can have our little secret. I'll tell you some of my secrets. Boy, have I got some you'll like! It's all part of life." He grabbed me as I backed off, started to kiss me, and gripped me harder and tighter. I felt his bulge. His breath was awful.

"No, no, let me go!"

***

He was incredibly strong. He raped me on his black leather couch, thrusting my face onto the cold chromium arm when I tried to bite him. He pulled up my skirt and ripped my panties. He said nothing until he finished. I got angrier and angrier as he thrust into me, and I got angrier still as nature took over, and I started to enjoy it. I do like rough sex.

"You know, it isn't rape when you squirt." He smiled at what he thought was a funny joke and a 'truth.' He was worse than disgusting. "You're a great fuck. Don't say anything. What I said is a deal. We both benefit. I know everything. You're a good slut. I want a slut. Marie doesn't even know how to fuck. Sluts are good. I even know about your pills. I have friends everywhere." He was right, I was a slut, and I was horrified. I was also in shock. "I know that you fucked Yevgeny the commie last night and this morning. So don't even think of trying a fast one. That guy is a loser. He has no money. He is a communist. Communists are losers. He maybe a good fuck, but fuck, he's a commie! I'm a better fuck, and I have

96

money. I have friends in the police. We are alike. Think about it. You like rough sex; I can tell." His eyes twinkled. He really was the devil. "We're partners now."

As I left his house, I looked across to the park, towards the tree where John had hung himself, and keyed his white Range Rover on the driveway – scoring deeply, with the hard chromium-coated key, the car's soft aluminium doors.

The speed of everything was going faster and faster. Back at my apartment, my anger had turned to revenge. You remember me telling you how I can work on the memory of a five-second dream and turn it into grand epic of War and Peace? Well, I had not yet begun to settle with Paul Senior. I called Christiaan and begged to meet me immediately.

"You have to go to the police, Helen!"

"I can't, Christiaan. I had sex with Yevgeny before I went over. I would be a hired whore to the jury." Poor Christiaan was speechless, his eyes wide open and his mouth agape. I was more than the things that were dreamt of in his philosophy, poor chap.

"Christiaan, if you have ever loved me, if you have ever liked me, even, you have to kill him! If there is only one thing you ever do, you have to kill that man. Push him off the ladder!"

I stormed off. Poor Christiaan. As I left, he looked at me in disbelief as though he had seen a ghost. I was embarrassed at my stupidity, the foolish games I had been playing, how I had orchestrated it myself, and perhaps worst of all, how upset I was at having been caught in these games and lies. And now a sweetie like Christiaan knew what I was really like. That was the worst thing. My pride had been stripped off, and the Empress had no clothes.

I had to see Yevgeny.

Why Buy the Cow When the Milk is Free? An Hour Later

Yevgeny met me at the Royal Conservatory.

"Let's walk on Philosopher's Walk, Yelena."

"OK," Behind the Royal Ontario Museum and the Royal Conservatory, there is a little curving path off Bloor St. where many a romantic stroll has occurred. We were not the first to have this conversation there. I told him I had been raped. He did not seem surprised or upset.

"Helen, will you marry me?"

"What? I am engaged – this is the ring he gave me!" Oh God. Another day, another proposal?

"I love you more than anything else in this world. Helen. Marry me!"

"Of course, we'll marry." I kissed and hugged him. "But what about Polina?"

"Well, I'll get you a ring right away, but it'll be smaller. I will be more famous than Paul. We can go to Venice on our honeymoon. Venice is great in the off season, when the fog rolls in the evening and as the mists lift in the mornings. I will be playing in famous orchestras, and we'll see Leningrad, Berlin, and London together…"

(Don't forget this was long before Leningrad went back to being called St. Petersburg).

"What about Polina?" I asked again.

"Oh, Polina is just useful. I love you."

Perhaps I could save my pride! Maybe I would be OK! Maybe I will be OK, I dreamed.

Denouement, Time Blurs

Some time passed. Hours? A day? It blurs. There was a way out, and my plans were firming. And now that Yevgeny had proposed…I could follow in Yevgeny's shadow and be his acolyte – it was the time to break off the engagement with Paul. Summoning my courage, I took a taxi to Roxborough Ave. Unannounced, I arrived just as the family was about to sit down for Sunday dinner. I told the taxicab to wait.

The father acted as though nothing had happened. But they could tell something was about to happen – Paul and I went into the dad's purpleheart wood-panelled study.

"Paul, it is not going to work. I want to break off the engagement."

"What?"

"I don't want to marry you."

"But…but…, what, you can't change your mind!"

"I have. Better now than five years from now. I am going. There is nothing that is going to change my mind. Please apologize to your parents."

I rushed out of the house without kissing him goodbye.

The taxi dropped me back at my apartment on St. George, and I rushed up the stairs to call Yevgeny to say it had been done.

"Is Yevgeny there?" I asked breathlessly.

"No, he's gone to Boston," Polina answered.

"Polina!" I exclaimed at her voice. "No, he isn't. I was just talking to him."

"He just left. He's accepted a position with the Boston Symphony Orchestra," she swelled with pleasure, ignoring, or unaware, of my shock. "He has been waiting for this position for months, and he just got the call today, so he's gone."

"Oh!" is all I could offer. Why hadn't he told me about this? "Do you know when he will be back?

"He is very excited. It was a bit of a surprise. We thought we were staying here for a while. Helen, there is something else I have to tell you. We're getting married! You're one of the first I am telling. We are getting married at our place on Cape Cod in June. I want you to be one of the bridesmaids. Can you come?"

"Wow – congratulations!" was all I could muster. He hasn't told Polina it is over with him? Gees, this guy was worse than me.

There was a hand-written message from Taliska shoved under the door. It said: "Haven't seen you in a while; give me a call, we're getting married!" Oh no! A multiplicity of weddings! There was a hand-drawn picture of a pussy cat with a giant heart and a jeroboam of wine beside her. A wine glass lay on its side by his tail, with wine spilling out. I've always kept it. What a contrast between my life and Taliska's; hers had continued her trajectory to motherhood and normalcy, and mine has just crashed, ended, kaput. Unlike many things I should have kept and have lost, I have kept this little reminder of Taliska:

A day, or a few days, it seemed like months, passed.

I called Polina again. "Can I have Yevgeny's phone number in Boston? He said he would call me." I am sure I sounded desperate.

"Helen, it has been in the papers for ages – draft dodgers can return to America; you know about the process, you know about his work with the TDAP, it takes time, the paperwork is complicated. And he told me not to give you his number."

So I rang off. Why isn't he calling me? Miss homebody was not going to help me. Yes, you know what is happening – but at the time, I didn't think for a second he was trying to avoid me.

Then I got the call. I thought it would be Yevgeny. It was Christiaan.

"Well, it's done."

"What's done?"

"He's dead. Like you said, he fell off the ladder. But the clock is fixed…"

"What? He's dead? He fell off the ladder?"

"Ya, I was surprised, too, how easy it was. He was way up…"

I hung up. Now, that was it. I was alone in the world, had not paid the rent, was failing school, had lost two boyfriends, two marriage proposals, and was now a murderer. Well, at least an accomplice to the murderer, and my accomplice was Billy Budd. He would not be good on the witness stand. Everything was black or white to Christaan. Oh my God! All I could think was: 'Struck dead by an angel of God! Yet the angel must hang!' The phone rang again, but I did not answer it. And I was too embarrassed to call my dear friend Taliska. My God, what would she think of me now? What would anyone think of me now?

Vancouver, 1981

Horace Greely had said to those 'barely holding on' to 'Go west!' I was barely holding on; I had let go. In such a short time, it seems, I had gone from the top of my game to the bottom. I certainly wasn't daydreaming dreamscapes based on my dreams. I had not seen my parents in years. I hated law school. We had moot law courts where I was praised for lying better than my confrères. The other students praised me for my performance at lying! The witness said "x," and it was my job to rebut "x" by twisting the words of the witness so that the witness thought had he not really just said "x," but rather really "y," and, as you all know, "y" was very close to what "z" did, not at all like, "x," so really "z" is innocent and is not a murderer after all…And we built a country on the twisting of arguments; no wonder politicians are lawyers – and are hated by you and me. The law students all clapped in unison at my clever lies and yet could not see what they were clapping for. I had to quit law school, that, at least, was clear. I couldn't handle the hypocrisy of the law and lawyers.

Of course, with the passage of years, I think differently of Yevgeny and Paul. The White Russian I loved and pined for, and who claimed he was mine forever, married Polina. Her name is Polina; I think it is a lovely name, sometimes short for Apollinariya, little Apollo, the rational, the ordered. But she called herself Elise. It was more exotic, I guess. I have followed them on Facebook. She was his Fuer Elise. The bagatelle is bewitching. The music rises and falls; asks, begs, turns away, seeks again; angers, rushes, trips, sinks into a revelry – clearly his real Elise had more than I did. Gentle and calm, pretty in her own way, she stroked and supported him over the years. Always there, lovingly building his fan pages, helping keep his demons at bay. High-strung, bipolar himself, he knew then – and I know now – I was not his harbour. I could never see what I needed to see. Now I am old enough to be glad he found happiness. We all fear the voices behind the door. Polina kept those voices away.

Paul was not for me, but he was kind, and, for a while at least, he loved me deeply. He was so different from the passionate Russian. His father was right; he was a naïve do-gooder with little imagination. At the time, I don't think he knew himself at all. At the time, I thought the sadness of losing me could envelop and comfort him. I hope it did. All that money had not helped him. What a family he came from. I don't know what he did or does; he is no longer on the rolls of the Law Society of Upper Canada – oh yes, they have changed its name now, is it the Law Society of Ontario now? Of course, deny the past with its history of warts and all, and instead of learning from mistakes to make a new and better future, assume you have already found a perfect future in Woke Canada. Paul was too simple to climb the ladder and become a judge.

All men perform differently. All my men tried to perform for me; never had one who wasn't trying his all. I feel sorry for men. I didn't have to do anything. I could just lie there. But I didn't. Secretly, I knew, intuitively, how to make men happy beyond their wildest dreams. Men are simple. All you need is to give them what they want.

But, of course, I was now alone. Again.

"Go West!" So, I did. As far as I could. At the beginning of the book, I included a map of Canada. It is an old map from 1921, and it provides an insight into the economic activities of the times. In some ways, very little has changed in 100 years. Canada is a huge country, and it goes on and on. Vancouver is painfully small. After all the travel and expanse across Canada, after miles and days of trees, lakes, rocks, prairies, and mountains, you arrive in such a small place. In half an hour, you have walked from one side to the other. You see the same people every day. Your life and your mind are like that; on the one hand, their possibilities seem limitless and expand beyond your imagination, and yet, at the same time, they are so contained, small, repetitive, and restrictive. A shadow seems to always fall upon our hopes and expectations.

Vancouver has mountains, the sea, rain, and the mist, and clouds. It is always overcast. Clouds are Vancouver; they are everywhere, every day, and they are alive, and they watch and control. They are the city's gods. They can be misty clouds that necklace around the mountains, thinning out to sea. Clouds that can be magical, bewitching, hiding secrets, and casting spells. When you look at the mountains and see those trailing wisps of clouds, waist-high to the mountains, they are inspirational in their beauty. But the next day they are oppressive, suffocatingly low overhead. Then they are a funereal pall. The day after that they are just higher, still dictating to you, blocking the sun. When the gods are happy, there can be clear blue skies; the mountains, and the sea beckon and all the world seems at rest. But most of the time, they are just ominous clouds, overhead, threatening, and raining. Forever raining.

***

I settled near False Creek. What a name! As its name suggests, it was not a creek but a small inlet. Back then, before Hong Kong money arrived, it was still industrial, polluted, and undesired. It has changed a great deal in forty years. I liked it more as it was. It had a purpose. It had jobs for real people. You worked, or you starved. And the mountains watched too. You were closer to the cycles of nature in those days.

Nowadays, Vancouver is a soulless place with a thousand faceless condos. People buy condos for investments, modern-day bond coupon-clippers. I suspect many live in China. Back then, I had rented a room on Hornby St. and had decided this was the street where I was going to start over. False Creek appealed to me as it looked a little less pretentious and less snobby than the north side. I also liked its name, False Creek. Knowing the difference between what is false and what is true is not always easy.

Those were easier times, and I found immediate employment at the False Creek Government Harbour. I don't even think he looked at me before interviewing me. He was desperate for help.

"Can you count and make change, Miss?" he asked.

"Yes."

"Your job will be to collect the berthage and locker fees, daily, monthly, and seasonally, as required. Some of the guys are a little rough, but they are hard workers and mean well. Can you start tomorrow?"

"Yes, sir!" That wasn't hard. My type of job interview.

It was a great job. I would walk the jetties daily, labelled A to E, the lockers E to A (arranged in an opposite manner to what you would expect), and learned the boats, the captains, and the type of fishing they did. To be taken seriously by the fishermen, you had to know the type of boat and the type of fishing they did. They liked that I asked them about their work. Now, of course, it is mostly luxury yachts, but back then, it was all a working wharf with fish sales to the public. I loved the fish smell and the working business of the nets and lines, the bilge pumping, and the upkeep. I memorized all the boats and their billing arrangements. It was not long before some of the fishermen just gave me their chequebooks and asked me to write out what they owed. I think they liked a young lady walking down the jetties talking to them; after a stint on the heaving swell, the smell of fish and diesel, I think they rather liked to see a young girl saunter down the wharf. And I was no snob. I was pretty - and I wore a plaid lumberjack shirt, jeans, and work boots, and they liked that. I was young, I had long hair, and I had, I confess, unbuttoned one more button on my blouse. A man likes to look at tits. After the heaving seas and the silver fishes, I am sure I was good to look at.

Mind you, the older ladies in the office were not so happy I got on so well with the fishermen. I don't think they ever walked out on the quays. It was not long before I liked a few of the fishermen. One drew me in, hook, line, and sinker. He was tall, muscular, and weather-beaten. Andy Begay. They said he was a native. What they meant, I believe, was that he was indigenous, not of Vancouver 'proper.' I remember the first time I saw him make a landing. I had been working for a month or so and already thought I knew everything and everyone. Everyone knew him and had expected his return. He was a character, well-liked and respected.

I went up to him as he tied up.

"I like your shrimp boat."

He looked at his boat and said nothing. But I saw his eyebrow move.

"My name is Helen, and I collect your berthage fees."

"Oh, I know who you are. They told me all about you over the radio."

"Well, at least I am trying."

"Andy is my name, but you know that already, as well as my crew and about my boat, too. You are quite a gal. Why are you working here?"

"Gotta pay the bills, Andy."

He smiled. I was making progress. The next day, I came to see him again, and he offered me a coffee out of one of his cups. It was some type of Nescafe, and it must have been made with eight tablespoons of coffee to each tablespoon of water. The cup was white on the outside but black on the inside. It had clearly never been cleaned. A spoon would have stood up straight in it. I drank it.

"The flavour improves with the years," I mused.

I complimented his catch. I asked him about smaller trolley boats. He clearly didn't expect me, know what to make of me, nor was he about to be drawn into conversation with someone new.

"What do you want?" he asked.

I don't know why I answered as I did, but I said, "I need a boyfriend."

He laughed. It was a genuine, deep-rooted, earthy laugh of someone who played no games and was what he appeared. He was the very salt of the sea. "Ok, I can be your boyfriend, but I'm a fisherman, and I am away for a month at a time."

Then he said, "You're a dark horse, Helen." I'll never forget that.

Fishing was new to me. There seemed to be larger, seine boats for shrimp and smaller trolley boats for salmon and tuna. Andy used large seine nets to surround and catch shrimp. These boats would stay out for a longer time and freeze their catch. The nets caught everything. Greenpeace would not like these boats. Trolley boats, on the other hand, were smaller, returned to port more frequently and seemed to require more of an art, a skill and a more mechanical process. It seemed to be more manly. I told Andy this and he would just laugh. Trolling the North Pacific for salmon, halibut and tuna was not a simple game. A trolley boat would deploy large arms hung over the ship's side, from which six lines would descend with individual nylon lines, complete with lures, flashers and sinks. So you can imagine the work and professionalism needed to deal with pulling in the lines with large halibut and salmon thrashing and jumping on the heaving swell.... this wasn't the RCYC boats of Lake Ontario. The Pacific is not Lake Ontario, either. Although Lake Ontario can be mean and cruel, it doesn't have the autumn mist, the smells, or the cold blowing wind from Alaska to Washington.

For two years, we were as husband and wife. I would meet him on his return to the harbour; bathe and clean him at my place, and then make love long and hard. A month at sea in a 60-foot boat with tons of shrimp would make any man stink. He was the biggest man I ever knew, and he ripped me. My doctor, Dr. Seymour, would make jokes about what his size and his athleticism did to me, warning me time and time again that he would not be able to keep sewing me up. I loved Andrew, the fisher.

All Andy knew was the autumn mist, the cold water, the bitter wind, and the longing for the landing. That and the diesel smell. I told him I wanted a real man who trolled instead of seine-fished, and he would just laugh. But even then, I knew, in the heart of my heart, that he danced to the tune of the sea and not to me.

At Sea Myself, 1983

I didn't have enough money. And frankly, although I had memorized which boats berthed where, what lockers the fishermen had, how and when they had paid which amounts, it was a rather simple job, and I was bored. A clerical job walking around smiling at fishermen was not what I wanted. I wanted something more. Maybe some Percodans would give me the apotheosis I was seeking?

I had been to the local bars with the fishermen and noticed the tips were good for the waitresses. But the bars were a little seedy. I asked one waitress one day, "You seem to make a good living. How hard is it?"

She replied, "With your looks, you should be working at the Atlas." We struck up a friendship. Her name was Molly. Andy didn't like to come to the pubs. We had begun to drift apart.

The Sea Dog Inn was not a classy joint, but the people were real. As I got to know the fishermen, I would go there more often. On Friday nights, there was sometimes a band. One night, a would-be Irish Rover band was playing, and I picked up a fiddle while they were taking a break. I had never played Irish and Scottish tunes, but luckily, I can pick up a tune easily. I had been drinking a bit and started playing the Fields of Athenry. It is a song that that audience there would like: people disenfranchised, who loved, had children to feed, and were thwarted by cruel authority. 'Our love was on the wing' – it is easy to bring a tear to the eye – especially if you bring out the vibrato on the fiddle with your wrist! I can't sing, but I play well. I do remember that night. Tips were good and appreciated. The regulars looked at me differently after that! And it was just, well, fun.

Soon, a man began to sing the words, and some others joined in at the chorus. Molly had tears in her eyes. Others were crying by the second time through the ballad. It was a big hit, and from then on, I often played a fiddle on a Friday night. That night, I seduced Molly.

Molly had brown hair, the softest milkmaid's skin, and a large bosom. Neither she nor I had ever been with a woman before. After a while, we moved in together, and my money problems slowly began to ebb. I paid off all my debts; even then, it had been hard to live on a government clerical wage. Andy had never had any money; diesel and the bank had seemed to take it all. I gave Andy cash I didn't have. I had watched Andy's shrimp boat head out for the last time.

Molly's brother had a scrap metal business. He came to the pub sometimes and would sing The Black Velvet Band when I played it. One day, he started to tell us about his need for tungsten carbide. Apparently, he could get a great price for it. He said there were broken drill bits at abandoned mine sites in northern British Columbia. It was more trouble to ship them out when they broke, so they were just chucked aside. This gave me an idea. I loved looking at the mountains; I'd love to see them up close. Robert had a pick-up truck he could lend Molly and me; we could drive north for three weeks in the autumn and collect tungsten carbide for him on holiday for us. We got maps, I researched mines for the last hundred years in British Columbia, chose mine sites, and it was decided. I was excited. This was to be my Washington trip (I told you about that before), stolen from me years ago.

We set out around the second week of October to catch the golden tamaracks and other autumn colours. It was a beautiful trip. It was lonely, too, out in the great outdoors. We slept in sleeping bags in the back of the pick-up truck, and it was getting cold. The great idea became less of a great idea as we found the abandoned mine sites empty of all scrap. Others must have already picked over the sites thoroughly. Fact is, we were using Geological Survey maps from Ottawa that had been printed in the '60s. These mines were long gone. Nature was clearly reclaiming what was hers. The sites were empty and quiet, and the voices long gone. After looking down dark and empty mine shafts, you could look up to the sky and see the infinite starry sky and the northern lights. It was grand.

And these starry nights are what I remember best. Far from the city, the sky at night was a mass of tiny specks of lights. So many stars they were numberless. You would look up, and all you would see were a million, million lights. When I was young, I found a book that had pictures in far-off times of a place in Italy, in Ravenna. They were pictures of the ceiling of the mausoleum of Galla Placidia. The ceiling was the sky, made of a mosaic depicting the countless stars in the sky. As a child, these stars made of little stones had captivated me. Growing up in a city, you did not see stars and the Milky Way. But here, out amongst the mountains and tall trees, you could look up, and suddenly, I understood that Byzantine artists captured the scene 1,500 years ago. Not only are we insignificant and our lives unimportant, but the whole earth is negligible, not even a speck of dust amongst the innumerable lightyear distances of the universe. The scope and size is, well, just beyond understanding. And to be looking for scraps of tungsten in abandoned, failed mines was just absurd.

The final straw to kill our great idea came one night. We were sitting around a campfire at dusk to keep warm (the days were becoming worryingly short, too), and Molly suddenly said, "Don't move! Don't say anything. Don't flinch."

I dared not move or turn my head; all I could do was to look at the terrified expression on Molly's face. Then she eventually said: "There is a bear behind you." For what seemed hours, I sat perfectly still. Eventually, finding us boring company, the bear wandered off. We had nothing to protect us, had not even thought about protecting ourselves, and had not even thought about wild animals. We had been fools and were unprepared to be somewhere near Prince Rupert, in the middle of nowhere, down long, pock-marked, unpaved, and winding lumber and mine allotment roads. I don't think many people had ever been in that bear's habitat. Canada is huge; it is so easy to get lost and disappear. We felt that we nearly did.

But it was beautiful out there. But with fears of bears, the increasing cold at night, and the complete emptiness of tungsten carbide scrap – or of any easily transportable iron scrap – we headed home down the highway. The journey home was as lovely as the journey north had been. Winding roads, mountains, hills up and hills down; sudden views, hidden creeks bursting into view, and giant boulders. It was the anthesis of boring, flat Northeastern Ontario. Little trees, big trees, gnarled old trees, and wind-tortured trees. It was the best time of my life. It could not last. It didn't.

We came back to Vancouver and settled back in the routine of old. But I was not happy at the False Creek Harbour. Andy was no longer part of my life, and I missed a man. For me, there is something missing with sex with a woman. It is a penis. Her brother was a male; he had one. Mine was the ultimate betrayal.

It wasn't totally my fault. Remember, Troy's walls never fell from the Greek onslaught; sly Odysseus tricked his way into Troy. It started innocently enough; Robert was a schemer, and Molly was too trusting. And I was too weak. Of course, I knew better. I learned some waitressing skills at the Sea Dog and then applied at the Atlas downtown. The Atlas was an expensive, classy place. Robert and Molly would both be out of place there. I knew I had to leave them and move on. But I did not move fast enough.

Robert's business was in Richmond, and he was busy. He didn't really have any business in False Creek. One day, he invited me down to his shop to show me the Thunderbird he was restoring. I knew what his intentions were without him saying them; I cannot deny it. I wanted him too. I must have made love to him five times each day for two days straight, making so much noise his workers just stared at me when we left after the weekend. His apartment was above the yard and garage, and you would have thought the wrecking noises would have drowned out my cries and moans. No such luck. I drove his Thunderbird. It was great.

Molly had packed my bags and put them by the door by the time I got back. She gave me a sterling reference for the Atlas, where I started immediately after giving notice at the government harbour. The owner at the Atlas, Angelo, asked me if I was playing in the Vancouver Symphony Orchestra. You could see where they played down the street from the Atlas. If only he knew what I was really like – or used to be. But then I didn't know what Angelo was up to, either. By the way, the Sea Dog Inn was the same distance to the Atlas as Hastings Street was from the Atlas. Hastings Street, named after a Rear Admiral in the Royal Navy, had been the most important street and historical centre of Vancouver. Now it is the centre of hard drugs and the home of the sad and forgotten.

Betrayal

1.

Is an ugly word.
It is long, harsh, and it trips over your tongue
Like a knife that jerks against a rib,
Slipping painfully, easily, deeply and up.
She sat there, looking at me,

While I talked excuses,
Enjoying my fear, as I waited.
"I've changed my mind," she said, smiling false.
She turned her head; the audience was over.
The promise, so quickly, was gone; worthless.
My hopes, plans and ambitions
Were nothing but phantoms.

2.

Being in love is danger, too;
A weakness; surrendering to another –
But love, passionately, consumes;
Unites; glorifies and makes whole.
And there is another difference, my friend.
A love lost is a love remembered,
The rejection, the loss, overwhelms, destroys;
But turn again to see the mountains left behind.
You see the glory, the vista, the awe of soaring crags,
The love you had, the memories, the moments
Irreplaceable; the glance she gave; the breast revealed;
Flowing in dreams of what was and might have been.

3.

Not so the erring loving partner,
She is empty, a cheat.
Luring to a chasm of greed and lies;
There is no redemption here.
The circles draw you in, down and in
To the centre of a ghostly hell.
You think she cares, trusts
And will, with honour, perform.

Fools, view the mountains behind!
Framed with the clouds above
Love alone is inexpressible, ineffable, resolute.
Forever one, real, eternal and only yours to lose.

Molly, being Molly, eventually forgave me. But it was years later. Robert I never talked to again. I was only a notch on his bed frame. But I hope you don't get angry with me if I tell you I don't regret that weekend of great sex.

The Atlas, 1984

Most people think only of Atlas as the long-suffering Titan who holds the world on his shoulders. But that is to simplify things. Atlas was much more than that. Like much of what is wrong with the world, complex, interdependent, uncertain and contradictory facts are simplified to a phrase or two, allowing them to be misunderstood or seen as one-dimensional.

Simplifications of complex ideas lead to hate and war. T.S. Eliot says, 'Humankind cannot bear too much reality.' Atlas carried the celestial spheres, which include not only the world and the stars but all of creation. He was the loyal lieutenant to Cronos, the youngest Titan, who, with the help of his mother Gaia, savagely ambushed his father Uranus, hacking off his genitals with the adamantine sickle made by Gaia and throwing them into the Mediterranean. His blood and semen formed Aphrodite, who came ashore at Cyprus…Cronos then proceeds to cut open his mother's womb, throwing Uranus and Gaia's unborn children into Tartarus, a deep abyss of torture and suffering. Nice stuff. His father, Uranus, not surprisingly, damned his son, saying that Cronos himself would be overthrown by his own children, the Olympians, the youngest who was Zeus, after a long ten-year war….and the story repeats itself with Cronos vomiting fully grown children, etc. It seems to me the ancients had a better understanding of how the world operates and what the desires and actions of men and women are than the hopeless platitudes and wishful thinking of the United Nations. Let's end world hunger and stop climate change – while starting a war here or there. The Greeks tell us what the world is really like. Their gods are really nasty. They are like humans.

But these myths of Atlas were far from Angelo's mind when he opened his club. It was a fancy, pretentious place where you dropped big notes and ordered fancy champagnes and Armagnacs to impress business associates. If you flirted with the men and wore a short skirt, the tips were even larger. It was a world apart from the Sea Dog, with its trays of draft beer and pickled eggs.

Angelo was the owner, a quiet, short Greek man; he called me 'Slim.' The name stuck, and soon everyone was calling me Slim. I liked him at first. He was the reason I took the job. Angelo was the brains behind the whole operation. You never got to know much about Angelo or what he did. If you did, I don't suppose it was good for you.

The General Manager was Ramiro, a Chilango from Mexico City. A huge thug of a man who was in love with himself. He thought he was God's gift to women and bragged about how many pounds "he could squat." He used his own profile as the model of the titan in the picture of the club outside. It was a garish sign, and I told him so. He expected the girls to service him if they wanted to get the best tables for their clients. Those poor girls had to give blow jobs to get better shifts. There was more money here than at the Sea Dog Inn, but blow jobs were the last thing Sea Dog waitresses had to think about there. I refused his advances, and he didn't like me at

122

all. It got much worse as his best clients would ask for me to wait on their tables, so I got the best times and tables without servicing him. This, of course, annoyed all the other girls. I was not developing friends where I needed them. But the tips were good and the customers rich and well behaved.

But sex between consenting adults for money was not the problem. A much bigger issue, I soon realized, was the drugs and the bent cops. The back entrance was off an alleyway, and I soon noticed the same cops going up the back stairs. One of them took a liking to me. O'Malley. Ramiro had connexions in Mexico City or Central America; I don't know which. But there was a large flow of drugs coming into Vancouver through this gang or conduit. Not the simple pills I liked for relief from boredom and the Curse, but the serious stuff with needles. This was the bad stuff. The people that were dying from overdoses. Not all drugs are the same. Needle stuff is the bad stuff.

People don't get it. Some people can handle pills; most can't. Some people can handle softer drugs and lead a normal life; most can't. It isn't a simple issue. Frankly, I am not sure drug injection sites are the answer. The users just sell the fake drugs to new users and then use that money to buy the real stuff. Why give free drugs to drug users, anyway? Why not give condoms to rapists? Give free condoms to rapists, and you lower the risk of spreading disease! The do-gooders never really think of the consequences of their actions. Once you are injecting yourself, you are a goner, and I am not sure there is a way back. You are toast. I am sorry for the people who have fallen even lower than I fell, but there must be some personal responsibility. We need to provide a way back for the bad cases with pills – but we can't stand back and let them inject themselves. Injection is the start of the end. That's my feeling, at any rate.

O'Malley was the name of the bad cop. There were others, but they were small fry compared to him. He was large, 40-ish, and had been a cop for some 20 years. He expected to get everything he wanted. He was entitled to it. He wanted me, and I said no, I was only a waitress. Luckily, Angelo even backed me up on this one. O'Malley was not the type of guy to take no for an answer. He knew all the tricks to hide his crimes. He loved to pick on the less fortunate. They didn't know how to respond. O'Malley's office was full of commendations from the media, the public, and his superiors. There were none from his victims. Most were dead. Women are weak and do not stand a chance against strong men. 'Twas ever thus. Only remember the native women murdered and ignored by the police, the media, and the judicial system. Those you heard of are only the edge of the misery and unfairness rampant in Vancouver. Don't forget Vancouver is the end of the line. The broken, the sad, the forgotten can't go any further west. Unfortunately for me, though, was the fact that although O'Malley the bent cop never touched me, he indirectly caused me great suffering. He, and his ilk, will haunt me forever.

Okomo was a short, wiry sort of guy with short, wiry hair. He was not a bouncer. At least, I don't think he was. I liked him despite his trying to watch the girls change in the hope of catching a glimpse

124

of their underwear and bare legs. He was paid cash to watch the back alley, and he liked that job as he also had a perfect view when the doors opened into the girls' changing room. Everyone said he was a petty thief and shoplifter and a ne'er do well. But I never saw him do anything worse than be a voyeur. I liked him as he seemed to be rather slow and gentle. His face was horribly scarred, he had very few teeth, and he often looked down, in embarrassment, if he could, to avoid shocking people with his face. He had a lot of tattoos on his arms and neck, which surprised me as he had very dark skin. He seemed to worship me, as I think I was the first person ever to talk to him directly. I have no idea what his age was, but there were grey hairs on his temple. I think he was older than he looked. When we were first introduced, I thought Angelo said his name was Nkomo. I called him Nkomo for ages until he corrected me one day when I was going home.

That night, as usual, I gave him loose change when I came off shift, saying, "Good morning, Nkomo," and smiled at him, thinking, of course, you never know when you might need help, so I should be nice to him. Unusually, that night, he was going home, too. Either I was late, or he was going off early. I forget which it was. But we walked out together. He was pleased I was walking with him. He put his cupped hand to his head and said simply, "You well, classy, Ma'am, my name is Okomo, not Nkomo."

In my typical flippant way, I replied, "Oh, I am sorry, Okomo" (I was carefully trying to say it slowly, exactly as he said it), "I get my consonant prefixes mixed up in Kwa-Swahili." Of course, I knew nothing about Kwa-Swahili or anything else about the Bantu languages. But he smiled when I said 'Kwa-Swahili.' At least I knew something! Here was a whitey that had at least heard of his language! He then opened up about his life in Zambia, formerly Northern Rhodesia, when he was a child. Thereafter, he always arranged his going home time with mine so we could walk home together. It was early in the morning, so I did not mind. I had moved back to Hornby St, which was on his route home, too. His accent was thick, and often, I pretended to understand what he was saying when I really didn't catch it all. It was late, and I was tired.

I do remember his tales of going hunting with his father for songbirds in Victoria Falls Park, where hunting was prohibited. The park was below the falls, where the first white explorers had built a village when they first arrived – and then died of malaria. That part of the park was haunted, he said – you could tell from the mists that rose in the morning and hung over the cemetery of "Rhodies" – as the whites were called – with graves overgrown with African olive and wild date palm trees. The townsfolk and his family hunted with his father's WWI Lee Enfield until there were no more birds in the park. He said it was such sadness. "The park was then so quiet." This quietness was in the dry season when the Victoria Falls were a trickle. In the rainy season, great mists rose with the roar from the Falls. The Falls were called "Musyotunya, the smoke that thunders," he told me, with awe in his eyes.

His father had served in the King's African Rifles, the KAR, of which he was very proud. It was Nyasaland in those days. I liked to hear him prattle on. His mother had kept his father's uniform, and they got it out every Remembrance Day and brushed it. He was very impressed with the red fez and the black cummerbund of the dress uniform. He grew up in Livingston, just above the Falls, and it was the capital for many years of what was to become Zambia. He was proud of his town. They were poor, often hungry, but knew, he said, what was important.

It just seemed so incongruous to be walking home so early in the morning, through deserted intersections with purposeless traffic lights blinking to no one, while listening to Okomo talk about "my kid brother peeing in the well" when he was leaving home to find work in the great Katanga copper belt of Northern Rhodesia. It was all so far away, so big, so grand, and different from rainy Vancouver.

One day, he brought me a casava root with such pride and excitement, and so I cooked him dinner, and we ate casava root by my window, with the mountains in the distance. Except for the casava, it was delicious, and we had a lovely time. And he talked of Ndola and Kitwe, northern mining towns on the edge of the copper belt, the decline of the copper mines when the South Africans left, the broken dreams after Independence, the sadness when the water stopped, and how the lights started to go out.

It was the way he described how he and his fellow workers tried to keep the cricket club going and how, in just a few years, the annual photograph on the wall of that year's winning team went from a nice, glass-framed picture to a picture, to a handwritten piece of paper on the wall, to writing the names of the players on the wall itself with a pencil.

He actually wept when he showed me the red cricket ball he had kept all those years. He was so much more than a voyeur.

Mon cœur s'ouvre à ta voix – My heart opens to your voice, 1986

One night at the Atlas, I had a problem with an obstreperous customer. It looked as though it was going to get ugly quickly. Before Ramiro came over (this was a fancy place, so Ramiro was often discreet), a very good-looking man came over from the bar and said something softly to him, and the loser left sheepishly and immediately.

"I see you have a lovely diamond ring in an unusual setting," he said as he turned back to me.

"Thank you, I am married," I replied with a safe answer; this was not an unusual pick-up line. His voice was deep, haunting even, and accent, though distinct, was unidentifiable.

"But the cut is not typically Canadian – or not generally made here. It could be Luk Fook, but it looks as though it is from Surat. Could it be from Belgium?"

"You could ask my husband, he travels a lot," I offered, trying not to encourage him, "Would you like a drink?" What was it about his voice, though, that drew me towards him?

"Don't mind if I do; Talisker and water, double. My name is Boaz. And yours?

"Mine is Ruth," I replied.

"Really?" There was something in his voice that made me think he was intrigued, knew the Biblical story, and knew, somehow intuitively, that my name wasn't likely to be Ruth.

"No, it's actually Helen." A smile then grew on his face. "Helen of the white arms?

Now, I was intrigued. It was unusual for a customer of the Atlas to throw out classical allusions. He sat down, and I saw that he had a pack of cigarillos. My type of guy, I thought. And he was attractive with broad shoulders. It was a quiet night, and I was not busy.

"What do you do?" I asked. "You look Jewish."

"I am a wholesale diamond merchant, yes, Jewish, and, like your husband" (here he winked at me – maybe he could see I was eagerly interested in him and that I was also trying to find out what type of man he was), "I travel the world. I do admire that setting and the stone." I wore Paul's diamond to keep men at bay. In fact, it was the only thing I had of his. Vancouver is not what I imagined big cities to be like. Customers generally behaved themselves when you told them you were married and working only as a waitress. So, the ring helped to keep preying men at bay. But it did not work on Boaz.

"Thank you, I replied. He had not taken his eyes off me.

I returned with his drink. "Passing through Vancouver on the way to Siam?" I asked.

"No, actually, I live here."

"Really, lots of diamonds here?"

"You'd be surprised."

"I don't buy your story. If you are rich and successful, flogging diamonds in India, Israel, and Belgium, why aren't you living in New York? Why are you in a backwater like Vancouver, in the middle of the wet and miserable winter?"

"You think I should read much of the night and go south in the winter?"

Wow! More fancy references! "Toronto has more money and more Jews," I replied.

He smiled, but he didn't answer. He never denied that he was NOT in the wholesale diamond trade, as he claimed. I never did find out what he really did. Diamonds might have been part of it, though. I wasn't going to let him off, though. What made him think he could just walk up to a drunk guy and make him leave quietly? Did he work here? Was he one of Angelo's or Ramiro's men? He was too classy and well-educated for that.

"I didn't realize they teach goy poets like Eliot at Diamond School. Where did you go to school, Boaz?" This guy was clearly interesting, and he was now my only customer.

"The Hasmonean Grammar School in London."

"London? You get around."

"I was one of the lucky ones. I was a baby on the last kindertransport to get out of Austria in 1939." Now I was hooked. Nicely older than me. I liked older men. He had clean, well-proportioned features and dark, straight hair. He was muscular with broad shoulders. And now he had an interesting past. And he didn't seem to be taking his eyes off my face. I especially liked that.

"Wow" was all I could say. I just stared at him.

"I never tip," he said.

"That's OK," I replied, "I give good service whether there is a tip or not."

"Can I buy you dinner the next free night you have?" He was interested. "You remind me of someone," he continued.

"Yes, please." I had already melted.

Anyone, though, frequenting the Atlas was not generally serving the public good. Especially politicians. But that is a story for another day. Here we had this good-looking, international "businessman" who appeared to be well-educated, asking me out on a date. He seemed a gentleman, but it was odd.

He drove a Jaguar. We argued; we discussed. We had great discussions. We kissed. His hand slipped into the pockets of my thin pants and caressed me between my legs. I squirmed and became wet. We kissed more, and I squirmed on the seat some more. He taught me how to kiss. I had never known what a good kiss was until then. It is an art, a practiced skill. And what it is to receive a good kiss! How I loved to give and receive such kisses! I could kiss all night!

At the right time, I slipped from his embrace and leaned over the console, separating the seats to give him a blow job. Men are simple creatures. The console between the seats is huge; reaching over it to perform a blow job in a Jaguar is hard. He loved it. I enjoyed pleasing him. He seemed much older than me – or had much more experience and knowledge. His wife was at least 20 years older than he was. He deserved that blow job just for teaching me the art of kissing.

Kissing begins slowly; it takes care, preparation, skill, and time. Gentleness is its hallmark. Planning to give and to receive the gentle impressions of the lips. The placing, the anticipation, the execution, the signalling, and receiving of cues are part of the art. The concentration on feeling and control of the subtle placing of the lips.... is a lovely experience. If only I had known the skill earlier!

Boaz lived in the British Properties. It was an amazing house with a great view of the city. One night, he drove me past his house. You could see the cameras on the walls outside; his wife was inside.

"How many diamonds do you keep in there?" I asked. I wasn't going to make it easy for him. I had already met his wife. They had been to the theatre and popped into the bar for a nightcap. He sat at his regular table to make sure I served him. I had known he was coming, so I was dressed to the nines. Miriam was positively old. And ugly. And wrinkled. Even her arms – complete with bat wings! – had the crepe look. Women age too quickly. I doubt she knew I was screwing her husband, but maybe she didn't care. For that matter, I doubt she was screwing him. He deserved more than her.

In fact, from her demeanour, I don't think she did. In fact, I bet she didn't know how to give a good screw to a man.

"Do you have sex with your wife?"

"No." Silence. "There is a chasm between us. There has never been sex."

"Why?"

"I had to marry, and there was Lakshmi."

"Lakshmi? Who is she?"

"A girl I loved deeply."

"She's brown!" You can't blame me. I was jealous.

"You're the last person I thought would say something like that."

"What happened to her?"

He ignored my question as we drove past the house. "A man is cursed to have an aged wife," I said.

"Yes, Helen, he is."

"Leave her and take me."

"You're not Jewish and don't know our ways."

"I can learn. All you need to do is pay a rabbi, and I am one."

"There are family obligations; there are generations of our family in the business. It is all related. We are all over the world. It was my duty to marry her. It is how we have managed to grow and maintain ourselves over the years. When there are problems in one place, we move to another. It is where the term 'the Wandering Jew' comes from. I had to marry Miriam. It was business. And, besides, my grandfather betrayed our family."

"What did he do?"

"To save his own life, he betrayed whole families to the Landesleiter. Austrian Nazis who were worse than German ones."

"What happened to him?"

"Oh, he ended up in the camps, too. But the others would have escaped."

He accelerated hard from the stop sign. I will never forget the engine note of the Jaguar. It starts as a low rumble, rising in pitch as the revolutions rose. Somehow, Boaz had a manual transmission in his XJ (most have automatics), and so you would have that burble in the engine note as revolutions dropped as he geared down to take a corner. It was a divine sound.

"I could become Jezebel the Jewess."

"You already are, Helen."

He did travel a lot; he would leave his Jag at my place, and I would drive him to the airport. I loved driving the Jag, and I hate to admit it, but I enjoyed the looks I got in it, too. With a manual transmission, I could blip the throttle on corners (double-declutching to the cognoscenti) and downshift coming up to traffic lights. It was fun pretending to be a racing car driver and to be more knowledgeable and sophisticated than the fat men looking at me from their boring Buicks! Then I would pick him up at the airport. Waiting has its reward, too. I wrote a poem about it. I grew to love him deeply, his mysterious comings and goings, his quietness, and his Tiparillos. Maybe it did not matter that I did not know what he did. He was strong and gentle. He could take command. I liked that.

Kiss me as you kissed me before

Meet me at the airport;
And kiss me as you kissed me before.
Meet me at the escalator;
And kiss me as you kissed me before.
A long, lingering, soft, kiss.
A kiss where your tongue gently licked
My lips, and then darted deeper.

Where are you,
Now that cold winds cut,
My hands chap, and the days shorten?
The golden leaves turn to brown
And scuttle, rasping, across the greying road.

Let me see your eyes sparkle,
Your head turn a little on its side,
And you smile and smile and smile.
I long for you.
Where is that voice that dances with your eyes?

A new life, a new struggle and a new search
For a new spring.

I will fight and return again.

Meet me at the airport;
And kiss me as you kissed me before.
Meet me at the escalator;
And kiss me as you kissed me before.
A long, lingering, soft, kiss.
A kiss where your tongue gently licked
My lips, and then darted deeper.
***

I do especially remember one time he suddenly turned to me out of the blue and said, "What are you searching for, Helen?"

"What do you mean?"

"We all are searching for something – whether we know it or not. A purpose. A dream or an ambition."

"What are you looking for, Boaz?"

"My family knows evil. We were even betrayed by our own family members. But Stalin and Hitler were external evils. They were easy to see. What we have now are growing internal evils that people just don't see. As the world gets smaller with more communication, more travel, and the increased standardization of culture, it becomes easier to influence and control the world. And evil gets larger as a result."

"I thought you sold diamonds."

"I do, and the contacts I have around the world not only help me sell diamonds but also help me to do my efforts to lessen some of the growing evil. What are you going to do with your talents and gifts, Helen?"

He Died in My Alley, 1989

One day, I was coming to the club early in the morning – not at a normal time. It was around five a.m., and I could see two figures as I approached. It was dark, and the lights had been turned off. Normally, the lights were only turned off for a drug delivery. But this was a Monday; shipments came in on the weekend. As I got nearer, I could see it was O'Malley, the big figure, and Okomo, the smaller figure, and they were fighting. O'Malley was shouting, "My money! I want my money!"

Okomo was whimpering and denying it. "I don't got it," or something like that. I had no intention of getting involved, but I thought if I showed up, at least it would stop. The pounding Okomo was taking was awful; the muffled thumps as the bully's fists landed loud from ten feet away. As I came up close behind him, I suddenly saw a revolver in O'Malley's hand, and he just calmly shot him in the face.

I saw the recoil of the gun in his hand. I saw what happened to Okomo's face. It just went flat and disappeared. I saw his body go instantly limp. I saw an expression of satisfaction grow on O'Malley's face. He smiled.

I turned and ran.

I called Boaz. "I just saw O'Malley shoot Okomo in the face; I know he saw me."

Boaz was deathly calm. "Where did this happen?"

"In the back alley. Just now. Not ten minutes ago."

"Don't go home; wait outside the lawcourts on Robson Square. Call me here in two hours' time."

In two hours, I called him back, and he said, "You were right. Everything will be OK by this afternoon. Are you at the lawcourts now?"

"Yes."

"Good; stay where you are, within sight of the doors of the lawcourts. There is a guard seated there, and he will watch for you. When the lawcourts open at ten, go in and sit on the chairs inside, all day, until they shut at five. By then you can go to work. I'll meet you at the club at eight p.m."

"You are sure?"

"Yes. I'll see you are eight. It is all taken care of."

"The Shield Unseen; thank you, Shin Bet." I felt better.

"Helen!" he said, clearly surprised. Then he seemed to check himself and said, "Knowledge is only useful if you know what to do with it. Otherwise, it is dangerous." Then he added, "Okomo had street smarts; I brought him back from Cairo. He was my eyes there. He worked in a gym. Doing a job for me in a Baladi, the Baltagiya pistol-whipped him badly. I had Vancouver General rebuild his face. He was a good man. He trusted you, Helen. That meant a lot to me." There was a pause. "The Atlas is more dangerous than you think. It may explode, deny knowledge of everything and anything if there are questions. I'll come at eight, sharp."

When I returned to the club that day, there was no body, but there was blood on the ground in little pools. I can still see the small puddles all these years later, looking at me. In all those little puddles, there were little pictures of what was left of his face reflected in it. It was awful then, and the image I see now is just as awful. That was all that was left of that man. I wrote a poem about O'Malley:

To Serve and Protect

He looked at the spreading pool of blood
And smiled.
Good shot, he thought. Banned dum-dum bullets,
Banned for the army, but legal for him,
Did a good job, he thought.
Blacks have a lot of blood.

He liked the feeling he got
When he pulled the trigger.
Such power. Such recoil.
The heavy weight of the gun;
The sudden heat; the noise.

But most of all he loved the whiners and
Complainers that would come.
He knew all the right lies; and the fools
Always believed the pablum provided.

Little did they really understand

Serving and Protecting
Was about his pension.

He put the knife in the contorted hand,
Pressing for fingerprints.
And gave a parting kick.

When I arrived at the club, Angelo was pacing nervously. I had never seen him so agitated. When he saw me (in the dressing room, I had put on a white blouse and my shortest skirt with shiny pantyhose to try and distract!), he walked up to me immediately and began talking quickly:

"Slim, have you seen Boaz today?"

"No, but he is coming at eight tonight."

"Nkomo has had an accident."

"An accident? What happened?"

"Trixie saw two men carry Nkomo away."

"Oh! You believe a story from Two Cocks?" I called Trixie 'Two Cocks' as she bragged that she liked to have two men at the same time, one above her and one below. While I like the idea of such play, I'd never been with a man who wanted another cock anywhere near his own or that would even lie close to another man naked, so I didn't think much of the men she liked.

"Listen, Slim! There is blood in the alleyway. A lot of blood."

142

"Gees! So, where is Trixie now?

"Trixie had to leave. She panicked; Angie has gone too."

"Hang on, business is good. I saw your liquor shipment come in yesterday. You're moving a lot of booze. Why would Daddy Long Legs disappear?" 'Daddy Long Legs' loved to cry "Daddy" out loud when she was with her men, had very long, good-looking legs, and was the nastiest for insulting and being rude to Okomo. I loathed her. She was the one who stirred up the girls against him.

"I think your boyfriend Boaz is involved."

"Well, count me out. I am leaving Boaz; he won't leave his wife." It was true; I was thinking of moving on.

"Slim, for a really smart girl, you are as dumb as Misti." Misti was retarded, and not that pretty – so I did not have a nickname for her. Angelo continued, "Ramiro is gone. too."

"Ramiro? Who's he running from?"

"This is no joke, Slim. We have product coming in tonight. We got problems."

"You mean you got problems, Angelo."

"You really know fuck-all, don't you, Slim? So fucking smart and yet so fucking dumb."

I just looked at him.

"I need Ramiro. O'Malley will be coming tomorrow."

"I don't like O'Malley." Angelo walked away.

When Boaz arrived, Angelo pigeonholed him before he could come and see me. I saw their animated conversation out of the corner of my eye. Anyway, I could wait as it was a busy night, the tips were good, and the skirt and nylons were doing the job of distracting my customers and my memory of seeing Okomo go limp. I could not get out of my mind the noise of the shot, the recoil of the gun in his hand, Okomo going limp, and the blood everywhere.

The next day, I read in the papers that O'Malley had 'accidentally' walked in front of a truck, dying instantly. Later, I found out Okomo was found floating at Reed Point in Port Moody, "heavily decomposed." When Boaz said he would handle things, he handled them.

That night, Boaz was kind and comforted me, but he said I should leave the Atlas tout de suite and that Angelo was "in deeper than he could handle." He continued:

"Helen, the drug cartels in Mexico are really bad news, and they were expanding fast up here, too. Faster than I expected."

"How do you know so much about them, my big man?" I said as I snuggled up beside him.

"The gangs reach everywhere. O'Malley was involved; I had Okomo watching him, and I guess O'Malley guessed it and took him out."

"Okomo was watching him? What the fuck! And he worked for you? What the fuck do you do, Boaz?"

"Dear Helen, I don't want you to get too close. It is too dangerous."

And that was all I could get. The next day, Angelo approached me as I tallied the cash and credit intake.

"Be my partner, Slim. You can have 10%."

"10%! Try 50%, skinflint."

"You can be my girl and have Angie's apartment. She's gone. Boaz says Ramiro flew to Mexico City, and by now he is probably hanging from an overpass. I need some brains on the floor, watching the girls, and I'm getting Juan for muscle when he comes with product."

"First of all, I like Esmeralda, she is cute, pretty, and funny, and you have two adorable children – so I'm not fucking you, let alone be your woman. Second of all, if Ramiro is gone, you're next, and third, who the fuck is Juan?"

"Think about it, Slim, it is a great opportunity."

"You think about it, Angelo. Stick to girls and booze."

Seeing my friend Okomo blown away was really bothering me. Not knowing what Boaz really did was also bothering me. I decided that my relationship with Boaz could go nowhere. I now realize this was the biggest mistake of my life. How could I be so smart at so many things and yet get the basic things so wrong? What is important in life? Knowing obtuse Greek metres, or having a man to share your bed? Sharing a breakfast together or understanding inverse kinematics? So often, I had bad judgement. No matter what he said, no matter what I said or tried to find out, I could not break the mysteries surrounding him. Instead of working within his constraints, I tried to push him. I was impatient. Although I was no longer young and should have known better, I made a big deal of his secretiveness. I wanted to know more about him and his business. Also, he wouldn't tell me about Lakshmi, an 'ex' that was not an 'ex' in his head. This really bothered me. I was a fool. I should have waited for him on his terms – he was smart, good-looking, put up with me – and, most importantly, he was the leader I had always wanted. I was looking for such a man. So why did I do what I did? He had even carved a little statue for me; carelessly, I have lost it, but I do have a picture of it:

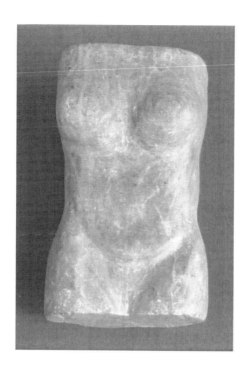

Where had he carved it? I hadn't known him to be artistic; when did he do it, and what was he thinking? Where did he do it? In a hotel room above some bar filled with geisha girls in Gangnam, Seoul, or on a beach in Madagascar, with the sun coming up and the morning ocean breeze rising? There is so much we do not know, never know, never even think of asking until it is too late. Then, we all have regret and sadness. And this has made me think of another side of Boaz, too. He could tell stories and weave whimsy and humour into them.

This was an age when you would hear that sound of letters falling onto the floor – a sound now gone and forgotten. And while those letters that fell could be bills – and was not always a happy sound, like a cork coming out of a wine bottle – Boaz would send

147

letters to me from far-off places I had never heard of, with little drawings like this one, a 'Linander,' a flying whale:

It was cute and fun! And so unexpected...he drew arctic piranhas too, but I have carelessly lost them, too. How ironic I treasure these memories more now than then...

Just one more comment about the arctic piranhas; he told me how they had migrated to Baffin Island after a family fight in the Amazon delta and evolved a white fur coat and four small lizard-like legs. Especially after I had done something I ought not to have done or left things undone that I ought to have done, he would tell me another episode of 'The Saga of the Arctic Piranha' as a sort of moral lesson. One of these stories I remember vividly was both horrifying and also so silly it was funny. The piranhas swarmed onto an ice floe as the mummy seals were singing lullabies to their white furry baby seals amidst a blowing gale, and the piranhas, with their rows of white, long, sharp nail-like teeth, formed a circle about the baby seals and carried one off...sniggering. It was just so absurd to visualize small Brazilian fish with legs and fur, sniggering to each other, while carrying off a thirty-pound baby seal. He even told how the indigenous would hunt arctic piranha by following the regurgitated furballs of their last meal.... you know, maybe Boaz's ability to see and appreciate absurd things was one of the reasons he was able to appreciate the innate goodness of Okomo when others could not...but what had been Okomo's mission – at Boaz's command – in a seedy bar in Cairo?

***

After a great night of sex, we often sat in his car in the parking lot by the water, watching the sun briefly appear on the mountains before it disappeared into the clouds above. The pink of the clouds was to be as fleeting as my happiness.

The clouds turned pink this morning
A blanket over the mountains;
The edge of the clouds grew brighter,
A golden halo formed around the mountains.
And then the magic was gone,
Cars pulled in beside us,
And the day began.

He said he wanted to set me up in an apartment so we could spend more time together. But I could not wait. I demanded an address now. I was still in too much of a hurry. Would a couple more years of experience have shown me? If only I had had more patience. Especially after my previous one-night flings at parties – great sex at the time, but so fleeting, and so unsatisfying afterwards – the sex in alleyways with guys I picked up because I could – often I did not even know their names – why would I NOT wait for him, and accept him as I found him? Now that I had found gold, why did I try to force him to move quickly? I knew he was under a great deal of stress at whatever his work was…But I never made the right decisions. Patience is a virtue, and I had little of that. I left him.

If only I could tell you more of Boaz. I wish I had not cheated on him, too.

***

As you know by now, the Atlas was a different world. It was downtown. Upstairs, organized crime spread drugs. Cops on the take would come up the stairs at the back. I tried to stay away from it all. But the old expression is that if you wrestle with a pig, you are going to get dirty – and the pig likes it.

The problem was I needed money to pay the rent and to live. And every decision I had made since heading out to Victoria College had been a mistake. I felt trapped and was going nowhere. I was worthless and felt inadequate. And Angelo started giving me Percodans. Worse, I accepted them. The issue came to a head when

Angelo approached me about doing a burglary on Boaz's house. He knew I was no longer seeing him. He wanted to know what I knew about his house and offered me a cut on the take. I told him Boaz would blow him away before he got across the threshold.

"Slim, I'll give you a cut on what we take," he repeated.

"Boaz? You're kidding! You and your boys are going to hit Boaz's house? You don't know a thing about Boaz and what he has and what you don't have, Angelo. He is a Big Jew, and you are not even a Little Jew. You need to look elsewhere. Don't make me laugh." Funny thing is, Angelo listened to me.

***

What else could I do? Accounting! Becoming a chartered accountant would not take much time; I had a degree and some of the courses under my belt already. Rupert Brooke had said Canada was a country of accountants. Though that was probably said as an insult. I applied part-time at the university for missing credits and sought employment at a C.A. firm.

An Interlude, 1990

I found the firm of Ted LeBlanc, C.A. He hired me on the spot. He said he doubted I would pass the finals, being an "artsie," but he would take me on as a bookkeeper; I told him I would make the honour roll. He laughed. I researched accounting and found Skinner's book on Accounting Theory. Other students-in-accounts were spending hours doing problems, studying prior exams and joining study groups. I read Skinner twice. Accounting is logical, straightforward, and boringly predictable. Once you know the theory (and have a modicum of common sense), it is a snap. The final accounting exam, the UFE, or uniform final examination, was only to see if you were honest and basically competent enough to hang up a shingle as a public accountant. It wasn't physics. Yes, I made the honour roll. Easily.

While I was getting my C.A., Ted started to take an interest in me. He had a Mercedes; Boaz's Jaguar was something else. A Jag's burled walnut dash was exquisite. Gauges stretched across the dash…it was just nice to look at and admire! It had class, looked expensive, and handmade. A Jaguar was class; a Mercedes was for the noveau riche, the type who would order the most expensive champagne as it had the highest price. A Mercedes may be expensive – and good quality – but its wood looks like cheap plastic. Why put a plastic finish on wood that makes the expensive wood look cheap? The car and its dash look utilitarian, single-purposed – like a well-made gas chamber. A Mercedes seems to have been made for the fat-bottomed German butcher who kept his thumb on the scale as he weighed your Schweinshaxn, that delicious pork knuckle. A Jaguar looked sensuous, with subtly refined but powerful lines. A Jaguar was for someone who had arrived and required a higher level of luxury, comfort, and handmade workmanship….even the engine idling sounded more manly when it accelerated, wow! A Jaguar pampered you. But, in a Mercedes, the centre console was lower, so it was easier to reach over to the driver to pleasure him….

Ted was divorced. His initial plans to use me as a competent bookkeeper gave way to realizing his clients preferred me to him. It was not hard to be more interesting to Ted's clients than Ted was himself. Early on, I was the bookkeeper and note-taker in a meeting with Ted's largest property developer, and Ted didn't know how to solve a problem. As luck would have it, we had just taken this issue in tax, so any other student in that course would have got it, too. So, uninvited, I said, "We could look at doing a section 85.1 rollover "reverse butterfly" transaction to get all the companies in one company, file, and then cause a year-end with another purchase by a "newco," and then butterfly out again with the new fair market values." Believe me, it sounds much cleverer than it really was. Ted's eyes lit up, and the client smiled.

I sensed this could be a problem with Ted's large ego, but thought, naively, I could manage him by getting more clients for him – and by making sure I did not make suggestions in front of clients in future. After a year, I moved in with him. This time, I had set up a separate bank account. I would need it.

Ted was everything Boaz was not. Boaz could run with the rich, the classy, the poor, the Atlas crowd, with anyone. He was confident and called himself, not with bravado but with understatement, "A Big Jew." Whatever he did, he did more than diamonds. He knew when to talk, when to act, when to get others to act – and when to lie doggo. Ted was insecure, hated change, had no open mind, knew little except accounting, and was not interested in improving his mind. Worse, he thought, since he was rich, he knew everything. He would have done nothing, I am sure, if Nazis came for his mother and his children. Well, he was an accountant. Cincinnatus was not an accountant. Accountants do not build countries – or save Rome like Cincinnatus.

At first, everything was great. He was considerate and supportive, people liked him, and I was bringing him clients. Then the jealousy started to grow. Then I started to see he was not what he appeared to be. At first, it was little things.

"Where has the dog gone?" I asked.

"Oh, he ran away," Ted replied.

"That's odd." We got another puppy, but I noticed the new puppy always seemed frightened of him.

He tried to manipulate me and others. He was socially awkward. I found him lying to me and to others. There was cruelty or negligence to his actions. He was impulsive. When I brought in a large account that he had not been able to land, and I suggested I take the Tax Specialty programme – which could double our billings – he got aggressive. When I questioned him on his response, there was a complete lack of remorse.

Then I found a handgun in the bedroom. The gun itself was fine; it didn't bother me that he had no licence for it. I am sure Boaz and Ramiro had handguns. A gun is for protection. But this is Canada, and accountants in Canada don't have handguns. He ignored my questions; it wasn't a normal response.

One day, I cooked a lovely dinner for him, his favourite. It was a pork tourtière following his mother's recipe with a Madame Benoit maple syrup apple crust for dessert. It took ages to make; he picked up the plate of the pie, walked over to the garbage bin, and dumped the plate and its contents, saying, "This is garbage." But it wasn't.

Then he hit me. I left. Problem was, I hadn't completed all my articling hours and was not quite a qualified C.A. He then called the police and accused me of theft – and told them I had opioids. O'Malley was gone, but who are you going to believe, the best-known C.A. in Vancouver, or a lady caught with opioids in a failed civil relationship?

As the court case moved forward, my lawyer asked for more money; I did not think he was competent and tried to change lawyers. These cases were not to be taken lightly, my lawyer guy was clearly incompetent and thought it child's play. It was anything but. At a hearing, he sent his junior clerk to court. This woman knew less than I did.

I called my parents for help and for money. My father said nothing; my mother: "You made your bed; now lie in it." My father was pathetic. My mother used to hit him, too, all those years ago. He should have hit her back. I hate spineless losers.

It got worse. The police got a search warrant and raided my apartment. They started to ask why I had left Toronto and about how I spent my time in Vancouver at the Atlas….

Then I got a lucky break. After a tough cross-examination, where the prosecutor was trying to trick me into one of those answers that would hang me – the very ones I had hated in law school – I said "No!" yet again to him, and then I turned and looked the judge straight in the eyes. The judge believed me, and I walked. I was lucky. But I had been really shaken by the whole process. God, the whole judicial process is brutal and cruel. If you are alone, poor, and innocent, chances are you are going to be found guilty. Who cares about the poor and the lonely?

In Vancouver, there is no Clarke Institute or CAMH. There is only the decline to Hastings Street on the East Side. And then The End. And Hornby St. was only a few streets away from the The End. 'Eli Eli Lama Sabachthani' – why hast thou forsaken me, a Christian might say. But I knew none anyway. A cold, empty sea wanted to swallow me. Or should I find a park bench on a cold night and take a large pot of sleeping pills? That was the best way to end it all – no mess. But Vancouver was not cold enough for this. That would work in Ottawa. But not here. I was a vulture feeding on myself. Why didn't I call Boaz? Or Angelo? Or even Molly? I don't know. Was it pride? I think I was frightened of letting others know what a total loser I was and that I would rather suffer....All I could think of was Joelle, a girl who lived in my building, who had lost her daughter, Alythea, to Children's Aid and was inconsolable. Joelle was also alone and abandoned. We had met in the laundry room, where she was shaking and quietly crying. Her entire eye sockets were red.

I guess I started to think more clearly of other people's limitations and capabilities when I met Joelle. Like Joelle, I had no one to help me. But the difference was, I began to realize that Joelle didn't have the drive, the hunger, the need to keep going, to never give up, that I had in spades without realizing it. So I tried to help her and in the process, I even felt better myself. Here was someone worse off than me that I could help!

I never knew Alythea or knew Joelle's full story. I didn't need to. I would walk with her down the corridors of our building; she did not like to go outside. She liked quiet company. Once or twice, I took her to her psychiatrist's appointment, and, somehow, we walked somewhere in the hospital where we weren't supposed to be, and a doctor stopped us – asking who we were. Joelle was, as usual, uncommunicative. I said we were the 'Les Misérables'. He laughed. But it was not funny.

I just feared ending up like Joelle. I thought of Alythea's soft and tiny hands, of what her laughs and eyes must have been like. And of the mountains of Vancouver, shrouded in clouds. Maybe Joelle could have written:

Alythea

That touch of your tiny hand, so soft,
Your lightening face when you saw my face!
The hypnotic gurgles of delight
Those darling eyes!

Never should I have left you
Prey to inattention
For thirty pieces of silver.

Now the mountains shroud you
With heavy, low clouds
Denying memories that might have been.

Not a chance had I.
Selfishness, past misdeeds hung me
A bullet through my brain
Homeless, faceless, friendless, wordless, nowhere to turn

If only, one day,
You can think of me
What you meant to me, and what I wanted for you

Moaning as the winds

Gusting, directionless, homeless
Longing for death.

I did try to help Joelle, but honestly, despair is not the answer. I remember telling her, time and time again:

"Joelle, you've got to get dressed in the morning. It is only a little thing. You can do it. You have to do it. You are not going to get over this if you don't wash. The little things are important. It is the first thing to do if you are going to get better. You can't stay in bed or in your PJs all day long. You have to try, one baby step at a time. Wash your face! Get dressed!"

You cannot wallow in self-pity and hopelessness. One step at a time. Little things. Get dressed! Wash! But there was only so much crying I could take. I am not cut out to be a nurse. You can't be a victim forever. I'm basically selfish. I began to see what my father had said when he said some deserters had 'L.M.F.' in the war. A 'lack of moral fibre.' Pull up your socks and get on with it. Yes, I know Spengler says optimism is cowardice, as the "Decline of the West" is assured and happening as we speak, but I think he was also saying you must manage that decline. Anyway, I wasn't going to have a nervous breakdown – or to try to hang myself. I climbed out of that drain, that Kierkegaardian 'sickness unto death,' that only one who has been there truly understands. But poor Joelle didn't have that internal strength I had.

I guess Joelle was the start of my conversion on the road to Damascus. Well, the start of one, anyway – it wasn't going to happen overnight. In fact, if it has happened at all, it has taken years. But I began to realize it wasn't always about me, really. There were others out there. And I could help some of them, like Joelle. Okomo's death woke me up to my selfishness and narcissism (well, it did seem that all men wanted to fuck me, so either I gave off vibes that I was a good fuck, or I really was hot, or both). Remember, I ran FROM helping Okomo. Okomo, who trusted me and was my friend.

Joelle also kept repeating a story about winning with her lottery tickets – but she seldom left her building, and I never saw her buy lottery tickets – but she had them all lined up in a little box. Talking about them was the only thing that seemed to lift her spirits.

I remember my Joelle's sparkling eyes,
And her excited speech,
Of how her lottery tickets

Were, one day, coming home in a
Three-masted schooner, at sunset,
With all the riches of the New World.

The tickets were all carefully filed
In a little brown box,
Row upon row.

I also started to look after her cat, Minette. She was a little black cat, and before I started to feed her, I think she was near death from neglect. She was only about seven or eight pounds and quite young. She bounced back with wet food and some dry crunchies, which I called croquettes, as she was a French cat. How did I know she was a French cat? Well, she said miaou rather than meow, for one thing. Joelle was from Lévis, on the south side of the St Lawrence, opposite Quebec City. Lévis has been French since they kicked the natives out (after they had been there 10,000 years) in the early 1640s and is well known in folklore for the story of "La Corriveau," a woman who was executed and then placed in a gibbet to rot for a few months by the conquering British in 1763. Apparently, she had repeatedly stabbed her husband to death with a horse-shit-covered pitchfork. But I think the popular story is that maybe she was not guilty, or maybe the husband was bad and so deserved to die. When do you determine someone is guilty enough to die – both the husband and his murderer? If I hadn't had to feed the little cat, I think I would have given up on Joelle. I am no saint, and she was pulling me down with her despair.

I decided to see a shrink myself. On the morning of my last appointment with her, a few months later, two pigeons were lovingly cooing on my windowsill as I got up, and I took this as a good omen. It was early spring, 7:30 a.m., and the rush of fresh, cool air on my cheeks made me triumphantly happy – and I could now hear other birds chirping, too. I looked out of the window. There was a young couple in the square below babbling on about something – it sounded as though he thought he was an expert on it, but she did add

161

some comments now and then. There was a little coffee shop open kitty-corner to my building on the street level. The barista was leaning on the door frame. A small motorbike, its exhaust dribbling, puttered modestly past. The scene was small, and little sunlight could dapple through the heavy foliage of the massive, aged chestnuts on Hornby St. The occasional splash of brilliant sunlight hit the balconies and shuttered windows opposite. If I looked up, the sky was a clear, pure azure, which, as an aside, is the colour of Zeus.

After my fresh coffee bowl of yoghurt, cashews, and sliced strawberries, I set off. Dr. Nadjiba de Llangollen. I had chosen her for her name. She had told me her father's name was Welsh, and he had been off the boat from Wales himself. I told her of her illustrious forbears, 'the Ladies of Llangollen,' that had not followed the public mores of the times. She had not heard of them. Two upper-class ladies lived scandalously and openly together and had many famous visitors, from the Duke of Wellington to Shelley. Wordsworth wrote a sonnet about them: "…Sisters in love, a love allowed to climb/Ev'n on this earth, above the reach of time." Well, knowing trivia has made my life more interesting. And there is nothing new under the sun. I bet they had great sex, too. Why are people so uptight about sex? Cats and dogs do it every day. Diogenes of Sinope used to masturbate in public in the Agora…why not? I liked to see men get a hard-on looking at me. I liked to give them a peek at my panties if I could get that look in their eyes.

"Pity," I had said. "I feel they were misunderstood, like me. May I also ask about your first name, too?" I had asked her at our first meeting.

"My mother was from Jammu and Kashmir." She always looked straight at me while she talked. She had stunningly penetrating eyes, and I had had a crush on her the minute I had seen her. Her hair fell to her shoulders, straight until curling slightly outwards as it rested upon her slightly sloping shoulders. She always wore white tops, had small, well-supported, almost thin and pointed breasts, and was slender, straight, and tall. I wanted to kiss her breasts. She had presence. Her nose was straight, and her complexion young and smooth. I don't think she was anywhere near 40; she seemed very mature and seasoned in her professionalism. I was besotted by her.

"Wow, Kashmir must be beautiful with the mountains and the valleys!" I had said to try and draw more out of her.

"It is beautiful, but there is no peace there, and my mother's family left for Canada."

"I had a teacher, of the Awans, in public school, in Ottawa, who was from Azad Kashmir, and he told me of the terrible fighting there after the partition. He was a lovely gentleman; he was trying to compile a dictionary of synonyms of Indo-European languages, from Nepali to Spanish. I was very impressed at the time. He told me the Awans were a noble tribe and originally mystic Sufis."

"There will be no peace there," the doctor had replied.

"Nadjiba is a Moslem name, and I was wondering what it meant?"

"It means 'assiduous,'" the doctor replied, "and my mother is a Hazaran. But returning to your childhood, did your father ever abuse you?" She, as her name suggested, would persevere and ignore my digressions.

I would have loved to learn more about her family as the Hazara are persecuted everywhere; often they are a Shi'a minority in a Sunni world, but my appointment was short, "Oh no, my father was totally asexual," I had told her.

She continued on, "Helen, you write in your summation of what you would like to do with your life that "the realization of my dreams will not bring me happiness."

"Yes, that's Tolstoy. He said we all make that mistake."

"You said you still think you have penis envy, too?"

"Well, I wanted to be a man. They have more fun."

"Helen, I don't think there is anything 'wrong' with you. My diagnosis is that you have adult ADHD. You exhibit some of the classic symptoms; a lack of focus, its opposite, a hyperfocus; a restlessness of activity and impulsive behaviour with its

164

accompanying mood swings. Also, you experience emotions intensely."

"Oh dear."

"Helen, you have gifts. You can see what many people cannot see. I think, though, a little medicine can help. Can you wean yourself off the opioids?

"I don't think that will be a problem. What medicine are you suggesting?"

"I also think your willpower can stop your use of opioids. Once you are off them, we will slowly introduce Ritalin, a stimulant."

"Oh great! Amphetamines! So now I can join Jim Morrison in Père Lachaise Cemetery?"

I took my last Percodan and went to the Pan Canadian Hotel. I wanted to have one last good time. Let me tell you, you have great sex when you are stoned.

Once more unto the breach, dear friends, once more, 2001

You have to remember that at over 40, I was still pretty. I didn't need lipstick, cleavage, nylons, or stockings to attract a man's attention. I wasn't married. I could do what I wanted to do. Loose jeans, a meaningful glance, and a careless smile still made some men drool. That night, I walked into the Cole Harbour Bar, sat down, and ordered a drink. It was an expensive bar, and I felt as though I wanted to go into an expensive bar. I was not well dressed, but I was wearing a large, brimmed hat of waxed cotton and black cotton overalls. I was dressed to stand out and to achieve what I wanted. There were three good-looking Americans sitting at a table, and they noticed me sitting by myself. They were in white shirts and suits with ties. They started to pay me attention. Then the waiter brought me a drink and said, "The gentlemen at the table over there said they would like to buy you a drink."

"Tell them thanks, please," I replied. I wasn't going to turn down a free drink. And three would be better than one. Maybe all at once, I thought.

"They also asked if they could come and join you?" he continued. "Sure," I said, nodding in their direction.

All three soon came over and sat down at my table.

They were lawyers from Seattle in town with some real estate deal. They were literate and well-educated. They were well-dressed and were celebrating the closing of their deal that day. They were staying at a fancy hotel, and they had boats, cottages, nice wives, and children. They were lovely men with happy, successful lives. They were funny, too. After more drinks, the eldest of the three made his move.

Drinks and drugs do not go together. Or, rather, they do.

"Would you like to come to my suite? It's a nice room, and the bar is closing here."

I never believe a woman when she says she didn't know what was going to happen when she went willingly to a man's room. "Sure," and turning to the youngest one there, I said "Better get three packs of Trojans before the pharmacies shut." He left quickly.

He did have a nice suite. Room service brought burgers, mixes, and some bottles. The most senior and eldest was plump, but in some ways, I like heavier men. We talked for a while. I got the sense they dreamed, but never expected, to get what they were about to get.

I laid down the ground rules; I put the condoms on them, only one was allowed in the bedroom at a time. I decided what was allowed, and I said when we were to stop. The others would have to sit out in the living room, watch TV, eat, drink, and listen to the action. I also said I was smoking between sessions. They were like school children given all the chocolate they could eat. Nice men are like soft pillows.

I think I gave them the time of their lives. When I was finished with the last of them, they could barely stand. They tried hard to please me, too. Believe me, all men are different, and I had a wonderful time. I smoked in the rooms – rather enjoying how much they would be charged for cleaning the room – and I know I was some Cleopatra to them. I know I looked cool. I was a movie actress from a Hollywood movie, and they were star-struck and in awe. It was a great feeling to be so desired, to give them what they wanted – and to be a source of such adulation by them. And believe me, I can provide the noises and action that men like.

They all saw me off in the taxi, tipping the driver handsomely, and the rosy-fingered dawn was breaking in the cool morning air as I headed off home. No, I did not take money from them. I had a great time, too. I bet they still talk about their night.

In fact, I wrote a poem about the three men while I was in the hospital waiting room, waiting for Joelle's death. She took the ultimate cop-out and killed herself the next week. It was quiet there and raining outside in wet, dreary Vancouver. As you will see, I took some liberties with my age, occupation, looks, and demeanour; it's called poetic licence. I imagine a black saxophonist in the bar:

Sappho's Apple

"You know,
Dad's money and connections gave us three
Our boats, dream jobs, doting wives, great kids;
So we were at the Coal Harbour Bar, of Pan-Canadian fame,
This band of brothers, drinking and laughing.
Everyone knew we were at the top of the game.

Then she walked in.

With a cocked, wide-brimmed, brown waxed hat,
In an all-black, size 5, cotton jumpsuit.
We stared. She smiled kindly.
We sent her a drink, and she waved us over.
And we stepped out of our world.

Salty, sun-sparkled, sea-spray her conversation was;

Her eyes danced, and lips were soft;
Her head tilted and smiled – we were thralls.
She listened to our bravado; she saw all
And indulged us, "Play on!" she laughed.
We breathed, we hoped, we tried.

But we swam beneath the waves, in the dark blue emptiness.

Time has slipped by, leaving long, quiet shadows
Around the day that was a life's adventure.
All we can now is wave down the years,
And envy the fortunate she loved.
If only...."

Sappho wrote a great poem about a ripe apple, which, like all of the best things in life that we want but cannot have, was in plain view, yet out of reach of the harvesters, on a bough far up on the tree. Like the apple, I was theirs for only a few hours. I know what men are like; whatever they have, they want more. But was I

Sappho's apple to the three of them, or were they, each, Sappho's apple for me?

This experience, though, marks a change in my life. Yes, they were loving puppies, licking my hand, and, at the time, they were putty. But it was time to move on. Je ne regrette rien. No, of course, I regret most things. But it is easy to deny fault, failure, and the obvious. Now I wanted something new. I wasn't sure what, and I realized the change would take time, but with Joelle, drugs, cigarettes, the Atlas, fishermen, I had had enough. Was I any wiser? I hope so.

I learned later that Joelle's daughter Alythea was raised by a solid, childless couple who had set up a trust fund for her. She had been dropped or injured as a child (there is a debate about how it happened and who did it – was it at childcare? Or did Joelle do it or allow it to happen through inattention?), and Alythea is slow. She works in a canteen assembling meals the way they do these days, with all the prepared foods coming out of various plastic bags. She never married. She lives with another girl and seems happy enough from a distance. I have not met her, though. I wonder if Alythea – or anyone – thinks about Joelle.

The social worker who put Joelle over the edge and accused her of hurting her own child was promoted time and time again. I see that she now has a blog where she talks about her course to re-educate men who are white and systemically racist. Apparently, there is a waiting list of men for her sessions.

***

For Joelle suicide was the escape. Hemingway killed himself after ECT treatment. I was certainly depressed walking down those long, empty hospital corridors of failure and remorse after Joelle passed. What can provide the substances – physical or metaphorical – that we need? Most of us are lonely.

After all these years, I now wrote to Taliska. As I have said, I was too embarrassed to tell her how I had screwed up and wasted my life. I didn't want to talk about my life. So, I asked about her parents, Adur, and her life. I wanted to learn about a normal and nice family. I wanted to sit back and read a letter of conventional life, filled with little worries about dentists, home life, and whether the daffodils would come up this year. I was tired of worrying that the over-eager guy's condom might break from his great pumping – and I didn't even know his name! It took me a while to find her address. Once I did, she replied immediately and quickly grasped that I didn't really want to talk about my mess. Taliska is lovely. She was there for me. And Adur, the dreamer, was just perfect for her. I was just happy reading about their journey through life. Taliska helped me get back on the path.

Charles Dickens had the companionship of his characters – many of them cartoons – which surrounded him, more so than the clamouring fans who fainted at his successful public readings that made him rich. Charles Dickens had been canny. He wrote at his comfy desk – with never a crumb or loose paper around – surrounded by his world of Victorian knickknacks, finely turned dark wood chairs, sideboards, leather-bound books in glassed oak cases, and quieting, woven, Axminster wool carpets. Meanwhile, with his tongue on his lip and a feathered pen in his hand, he was comfortably creating worlds like Fagin's stark cell the night before his execution at Newgate. Fagin sits on a stone bench in the dark, pilloried and wounded from the objects thrown at him, ruminating on his coming execution in the morn. Of course, Dickens was heralded as a genius! He kept a perspective, a distance, from his own personal world and the worlds he created. His creations captured the imagination of an age – he observed and described human nature, transcribing it so others could appreciate his vision.

Compare Dickens, famous for writing fiction, to me, an unknown, recounting actual life (I wish it were fiction!) – with a chewed and leaking ballpoint pen in hand. And I am writing a poem about three men doing a woman in a hotel room while sitting on an uncomfortable steel and plastic chair in a hospital waiting room, sheltering from the Vancouver drizzle, waiting to hear if your friend is pronounced dead, and imagining not made-up characters like Dickens, but of hiding from real people I had hurt. 'Du sublime au ridicule il n'y a qu'un pas —, but a step from the sublime to the ridiculous,' Napoleon, of all people, had said this on his retreat that degenerated into a rout from Moscow. My life indeed.

Shortly afterwards Joelle was buried – in a pauper's grave at Surrey Centre Cemetery – Minette suddenly took a turn for the worse and died. I have no idea why this happened. The little cat's unexpected death upset me more than Joelle's had. Perhaps, despite being starved by her, the little cat could not live without Joelle.

Those little eyes,
And that little head,
Turned up to me
Searching,
Asking, begging,
"Please help me!
I know I am dying, and you have always helped me,
Fed me,
Cuddled with me
and whispered cat-things to me while
we snuggled,
so nicely,
that I loved so much, oh
Please help me now that I need so much help,
Oh it hurts so much,
Please help me!"
Oh poor puss!
Your breathing's so shallow,
Oh you are so little, my dear, little, Minette.
I can't help you my lovely cat.
At the end I failed you and could not help you.
Poor Pussy.

The therapy sessions had served their purpose, I had quit drugs and cigarettes. But if I could not have a relationship with the doctor, I did not want to see her again. Yes, I am self-destructive as well as a contrarian. I was bored, felt worthless, knew I was a failure and yet needed excitement. So I started to develop my daydreams again; now they always seemed to portray disaster; always, they seemed to have, more or less, the same plot.

Armageddon, 146 BC

The Saka were continuing to sweep down from the mountain passes. The Silk Road was no longer a route of merchants, rich goods, and caravans. As I looked out from the palace windows, I could see nothing but a long trail of oxen carts, with huddled figures and a few goats and cattle trampling alongside them. In the distance, I could see smoke rising straight up towards the sky from burning villages. What would keep Alexandria on the Oxus alive? It would soon fall. There was nothing to stop the tide. There was that horrible feeling it was about to end and there was nothing I could do. Quite literally, I was a spectator of my own demise.

As I looked out below, all I could see were more mouths to feed as the flow of weeping children, bleating goats, and sullen men wound its way up to the gate and into our city.

Why wouldn't my brother Antiochus fight them? There was to be another meeting of the Council of the Wise this afternoon. I would attend today and no longer would I stand by and say nothing. I was a Queen. I would be called when the clepsydra, the water clock, ran out. Until then, I stared at the unmoving mountains and watched the winding trail of misery.

When I arrived, the bell had only just stopped tolling, but the meeting had already started. The Haruspices were there, in their dark robes, surrounded by the tools of their trade. The bronze liver from Hattusa and the Akkadian clay models from Babylon, covered in their cuneiform inscriptions, were upon the dais with the freshly examined sheep's and goats' livers – even a bull's liver. From the expressions on the priests' faces, it was clear that they all agreed upon the divination, and the prognosis was not good.

"What do the gods command? I asked of Antiochus.

"All the livers are rough and shrunken; look, even the bull's liver is missing the head of the liver, the lobes are twisted and the river of life, the portal vein, is blocked. Anger has agitated the bile; there is no brightness; no dappled symmetry, no smoothness, fear has drained the liver, leaving it shrunken, dark, a slave to the coming catastrophe." replied Pammenes, Chief Priest and Haruspex of Balkh.

"Why do we care what the barbarians we conquered believe?" I asked, turning to Antiochus. "They are not our priests. They do not live here; they could be taking their fees from the Saka themselves and you would not know it! They don't even speak Greek!"

"Sister, there is an oracle, too, the oracle of Didyma,"

"But that was a good oracle – it referred to you and your triumph over the Sogdians."

"Yes, but the Saka are unlike other barbarians; they are not Sogdians. They are like us; they are foreigners in this land. We cannot fight them and win. The gods are against us."

"This is nonsense! Thousands of your citizens are fleeing their burning homes and fields, and you cannot fight the Saka as they are foreigners? Better to come home upon your shield than to throw down your shield! Brother and husband, you cannot stand by and let your kingdom collapse! At this minute thousands of your fleeing citizens seek your help – outside your very windows! This is our inheritance!"

"The gods have spoken," and Antiochus walked away. He had despaired and had given up. Even in my dreams I don't like people who give up.

***

A repeating image I had was of the actual sacking of the city. I was Cleopatra Thea once again, fleeing my palace, down the hill from the citadel, through the flag-stoned burning streets of Alexandria, holding little Thaïs' hand, wearing either a long white stola and tunic or, perhaps more believably, in peasant attire in rough sackcloth, past the putrid, nauseating, steaky smell of burning bodies of animals and men, with burning embers drifting in the hot air, singeing my hair and face as the city burned. Screams and cries were everywhere; metal on metal clashed; the crackle of flames surrounded us. Suffocating black smoke wafted from the burning pitch of the rooves, choking us. Past perpendicular white marble Corinthian columns with contrasting horizontal, long cedar timbers, seemingly alive as they burned with flickering flames and blackened. Cedar resins…that intoxicating resin smell; earthy, spicy, burning; drifting to your nose and then away, a lovely smell; relaxing, exhilarating, yet redolent of Pharaonic death, mummification, and rebirth…nothing matched the smell of those resins! Gilgamesh was right to think of how the tall and great forests of cedars surmount mortality, leading to eternity… that vision of fleeing the burning city, and the smell of burnt flesh, will forever haunt me….

The Saka had taken Antiochus' land and, with it, my desperate hopes.

Part III

The Long Deep Summoning of the Supper Horn

Sir Charles George Douglas Roberts, The Potato Harvest

This great Canadian poet understands our need to fuse our disparate longings with the contradictions of work, duty, and love. He sees both the frenzied panic of our fleeting lives and that eternal stillness around us – the harvest, the slow-wheeling hawk high above, and the wind-blown marsh reeds – and offers us a path with a view of Home. The journey can be long and hard, with detours and dead ends, and the destination may be unknown and even unrecognized when found. But we all hear the calling. Illusions or not, understood or not, we want the memories of the vagaries of chance and change – and a home.

Halifax, 2006

It was time for me to retreat, too. The opportunity came at the most unexpected place. While waiting in line at the drugstore, I picked up a copy of Macleans. It was time to head back east. Vancouver was done for me as Toronto had been before. It was time for a new Loony Bin. At the time, Facebook was coming alive, and I tried to reach out to those I thought might help me. It was depressing; some of them were dead. I found Hendrik and contacted him. Hendrik was a farmer; he had married a farmer's daughter, and they now lived in Sheddon, Ontario, the 'Rhubarb Capital of Canada.'

"I run the Rosy Rhubarb Festival every year," he laughed over the telephone. "My company is called Riley's Rhubarb," he continued.

"Do you have children?"

"Yes, four, all boys."

"Are they like you?"

"Nope. Something went wrong. They are all nice kids…"

"I think they broke the mould."

I didn't think Hendrik would be able to help me. I got the impression his wife kept a tight rein on him, and he liked it that way. I moved on down my list.

Depressed by all the success stories and happy lives and families of people I knew on Facebook, I picked up the Maclean's magazine I had bought. I fell out of my chair. Beatrix Andrewes, a girl I was in Annesley Hall with, was now the priestess-in-charge at the Halifax Stone Church. Well, she will remember me! I will go and visit her.

***

It was late August, and dawn was coming later. On the bus trip from the airport, we passed hungry, small, parched trees, seemingly trying to scratch a living beside still silver lakes of reflected clouds. The rough scrubland and small lakes seemed so far away from the vast mountains and tall trees of British Columbia. Things did not bode well. Was this a wasteland I was heading into?

Hotels were not cheap and were, anyway, out of my price range. I played the hard-up card and received much-needed help from a small charity that helps women with temporary housing. I am glad I am not a homeless man. The sexes are not, and have never been, nor will they ever be, equal. The place was nice, clean, and extremely cheap, but there was no privacy, and the four "guests" shared everything - from the TV to the bathroom. Well, not quite. We did have separate beds! And it was close to the water.

I got up to watch the dawn over the bay. I walked down to the boardwalk, past HMCS Sackville, and sat on a bench. It was warm, there was no one about, and there was yet no colour in the sky. I wanted a new beginning here - or at least some advice. Watching the flicking lights on the Dartmouth side, I wrote:

In the dark blue quietness, lights from across the bay shoot across the wave tops, dancing.
As dawn's vermillion grasps the horizon, the calm sea resolves.
The ocean's breath awakens and brushes my cheeks.
I breathe deeply; the cool air's saltiness fills my lungs and tingles my nose.

Aurora is born! The sky pinks and fades; its duty done.
Gulls cry, and sweep low over the soft, undulating swell.
Others answer from afar; some climb high into the sky to reach the whitening clouds.

The waning moon dulls,
The water lightens, copying the lighting sky, twins together, in matching, silver blue.
A few high, high, clouds seek 'Ouranos, father of the Titans himself.
Like a dawn gun booming, the first ferry's foghorn rolls across.

The sky turn orange, then yellow, widening, across the bay.
Sea and sky's yellow bands unite - and then a lady walks by, Smoking.

Her cigarette smoke, strangely comforting, trails behind and is gone.
The ferry's diesel cuts as the quay approaches, and the day begins.

As a child I had read a book on the Titanic, one that contained pictures of some of the drowned children who were buried in Halifax cemetery. The photographs had their eyes open, but the salt water had destroyed the cornea. So where eyeballs were supposed to be were only opaque whiteness staring back at me. It had terrified me. I had been the same age as one of the girls in the picture. There she was, staring back at me, unseeing. My life, indeed. I had to go to the cemetery, find the graves, and pay my respects. I did find their graves, quite by accident. A quiet and neglected spot amidst the city's bustle. The grass was long by the gravestones. How the world had been possessed by the great ship's sinking, and how the victims were all forgotten now. I returned to the hostel.

Halifax was a big improvement over my time in Vancouver. Maybe it was just the change of scene I needed. After a few days, I had had enough of my hostel. The people in the hostel were "nice," but it was that sort of place where everyone had issues. One lady could not go outside; another thought people were looking at her, and they all sat in the main room and watched T.V. Yes, I have problems, but I am too selfish to make allowances and talk to them. I wanted to get away from them. So, collecting the front door key from the lady at the desk (who always talked to herself (Gandalf talked to himself – a habit of the wise, he said, they choose the most intelligent person present to talk to), and headed to Beatrix's Church.

Beatrix Andrewes had been slim at Annesley Hall. That was thirty years ago. In the article in Maclean's magazine, she was large. Very large. Benvolio calls out to Mercutio and Romeo, "A sail, a sail," when he sees the fat nurse, and truly, that is what Beatrix in that pic looked like at her altar. I wondered if me calling her "Lancelot" all those years ago had inspired her to join Holy Orders? I had read the poem "The Magi" to her in the Common Room. But she would not have known about Lancelot Andrewes, her last name's forbear, whose brilliant sermons had inspired T.S. Eliot's poem. At the time, I was not sure she was even listening. How incongruous life's turns can be!

She had invited me for noon, but I came for an earlier Matins service; there were three or four old 'wrinklies' in the pews for the weekday service. I let the wrinklies say goodbye, first of all, to the priestess. When they had left, she greeted me and seemed pleased to see me, inviting me back to the rectory. We waited until the regulars were out of earshot.

"Oh, it is great to see you, Helen! My, it has been a long time! Too long…...!"

"This is a conservative parish, Beatrix."

"Yes, I have found people like tradition and ritual. They need something to hold onto, to give them meaning. This Church is alive; it uses the Book of Common Prayer."

"But that talks about priests rather than priestesses, Beatrix! How do you fit into that?"

"You always jumped to the quick, Helen," she laughed, "Let's wander off to the rectory."

She continued as we walked, "Islam is growing as it demands something of you; Ramadan is not hard to follow – yet it is

184

something – and yet most Churches these days demand nothing of you. You need to have something demanded of you. In fact, you choose what you want to believe these days, and thus most denominations are dying. That is our problem. We need to stand for something. Can you imagine an Iman standing up at Friday Prayers and saying it is OK to draw pictures of Allah? Of course not. But it is OK to say Jesus was transgendered in a sermon or that Jesus is nothing but a good man…Offer us nothing, and we take nothing. Offer the absurd, and you get less than nothing. And as for women priests, well, we go through our lives, and we sicken, and then we die. We are mortal. How important is it that our priests are men or women, if we all going to die? It is the rebirth that is important. What I find in my parish is loneliness. Most are lonely. Lonely for the Holy Spirit and for other people. Company. People want company. I just try to do my little bit. Eventuality means we must make compromises when the time comes. Priests or priestesses? They aren't what is important on Judgement Day. As you see, most of the congregation is elderly – as we get older, our mortality becomes more important, our weaknesses greater, and our needs for salvation loom larger. Our sins grow larger in our memories. So, the people of this parish have accepted me despite my gender - or maybe because of my gender? Perhaps the men they had as priests before left a gnawing hole in them? Did the male priests they had believe in the Creed? I think they chose me to be their priest as I speak of the Gospel as a light yoke, but one that says you must BELIEVE, to choose. Not with the "*spirit* of the Creed"; but, *believe* the words of the Creed. There is a difference, you know…"

"Ah, the Kierkegaardian leap of faith into the hands of an infinite and loving God…"

"…Yes, come, let us go into what I call my garden room…"

Conversation then turned to pleasantries – she did spend too long complimenting my clothes and my appearance – and we sat down to tea. Luckily, there was a wide loveseat for her to sit on. I sat on a small, low, chair, one that could twirl with my foot to the left and right as we chatted. A 1960s chair, I thought, in an ugly pale gold shade. The room's furniture did not look as though it had changed in 50 years.

"Where are you staying? You must stay with me. Are you travelling with anyone? What HAVE you been doing? I haven't seen you since 1979…."

I was only too happy to leave the charity room with its "transitional" housing arrangements – and move into Beatrix's spare bedroom. Guiltily, I was hanging onto some pride. I was poor, but not so poor to have lost all self-respect. And I wanted to tell my story. I wanted to continue to be selfish and to talk about myself.

***

After I had spent hours over a number of days telling of my travails and failures, and we had just washed up the dishes together, I turned to her and said, "But Beatrix, you haven't told me about what you have been doing." It was odd that she had told me nothing about herself and just kept asking me questions. I had bought some bottles of cheap bubbly wine down the street – I did not want to start drinking her sacramental wine – and poured some for her as we moved to her 'garden room' with the windows overlooking the flowerbeds. On the windowsill, enjoying the late afternoon sun, was a fragrant gardenia blooming. The smell was intense, perfect, the perfume of the gods. It was a Cape Jasmine, the best and most intoxicating of all gardenias…its glorious white, waxy petals wantonly open to seduce all who came near. Once you have smelt it, you will never forget that divine smell!

And then she started. "You asked me about my life, Helen. I was raped. It sounds almost flippant to talk to about it. He is on VICLAS. You know VICLAs? The violent crimes linkage system? The officer found my story credible. The whole affair seems unreal. I was full of shame, thinking it was my fault because I was not mentally present. Believe me, I was very far away. It was all dissociation; I was not in the room. I was humiliated. I tried to keep it all under wraps. Do you understand? Helen, you quite simply have no idea of the depravity of this fellow – even if I were to tell you. You can't understand this, but I cannot turn the verbal fountain on and off, at will, especially under time pressure. It is a trauma, a life-affecting event for me. Non, non, non, as the French like to say. I spent - I know it's a big country – but this was a big crime affecting ME! Years! It took him hours to overwhelm me; asking me questions about my life, telling me about his life, all the while trying to overpower me by holding my arms behind my back and

187

talking….it was a game he was playing, wearing me down. And tearing my clothes off. Do you understand? I was new to men; I didn't know; I trusted him. How can I trust a man? For years, I had nightmares. He was tearing my clothes off! The therapists could do nothing to help. They just sat there and nodded. They did nothing! It repeats; the whole affair kept repeating. All the expensive therapists cared; they meant well, but they did nothing. They were useless. It was my life. Not theirs' – or his. They could do nothing. It wasn't until I joined the Church that the nightmares faded. That was some twenty years ago. It wasn't until I had done that, that my nightmares faded. That's why I went to the Church. I could not cope. It was torturing me. So, yes, prayer helped - but I had to listen to the Holy Spirit."

She certainly had had a different experience with men than I had had. She was really scared of men for life. Over the next few weeks, we would chat about her horror as well as my mistakes and misadventures, and she was wonderfully sympathetic and supportive. I stayed away from what happened between Emerson Senior and me. I think I was still blaming myself for having gotten in that position in the first place.

I felt Beatrix was just innocent and naïve. She had gone on:

"My parents had rented an apartment in Village by the Grange – do you remember the place?" I nodded, "and I had got a job at the Art Gallery of Ontario; I had just graduated. I met a Tunisian student there – Ahmed Omar – whose parents were in the tile business. I loved the tiles. I thought we were just friends. I did not expect what happened. It was a betrayal."

And then she added, "It seems so odd you do not know."

"Why? How could I know about the dreadful time you had?" I asked. "I always had great sex and great experiences with men."

"Come, Helen, you ran off to Vancouver after two of them jilted you. You deny your own suffering. You just told me their story. I remember Paul. I knew you were dating him and thought you were lucky to have found such a nice boy who was so wealthy. I was jealous of you. He seemed such a nice guy. Son of a famous rich Rosedale tycoon. What more could you want? I followed the story in the papers. Sad the father died of a heart attack or something. There was a man with him at the time."

"Beatrix, he didn't fall off the ladder. He was pushed." I don't know why I admitted it then. But I did. "Oh yes, it was murder, Beatrix. The father had raped me, and I had another boyfriend push him off the ladder in revenge. I didn't tell you that bit. Christiaan de Klerk. He had known me in Ottawa in high school. Christiaan staged it to make it look like an accident. He helped me get revenge."

"Murder? Don't be silly and dramatic. No, no, I remember this. He died of a heart attack or something – it wasn't murder. I am sure it was an accident. Did you talk to him afterwards? I remember the name now, it was in the papers, 'Christiaan.'"

"Oh no, I have never since been in touch with him."

"You should. There was something wrong with the man's heart; he fell off the ladder after the heart attack – there was an autopsy. You are projecting guilt, Helen. Anyway, someone who would kill for love is not someone to have thrown aside so easily, Helen. You, of all people, should know that. And what is this about the father raping you?"

I told her my sordid details. Beatrix thought I was a nicer person than I was. She was soon thinking it was all Paul Senior. He had made me kill him. As evil as I was and as evil as Paul's father was, getting someone to kill him was the worst thing I had ever done, and I could not deal with it. And Beatrix seemed to ignore what I had done. She seemed to make light of it. Or not believe me.

She sat next to me and drank more wine. We had more in common after my confession. And I kept filling her glass. We got comfortable. After she kissed me, my hand went around her, and I undid her bra. There was a lot of sweat under her breasts. Things progressed, and after taking her panties off, I lifted her panniculus to pleasure her and my arm disappeared up to my elbow before I reached the spot.

I had weird dreams that night. I heard owls hooting. I could see only rows of elderly people in the pews in the Church. Somehow, I knew they were all lonely and that they all had stories to tell of both sadness and happiness. The dream ended with a blue heron flying overhead. In the morning, I told Beatrix I had to leave.

That morning, before she woke, I went through Beatrix's wallet and took all of her bank notes. I felt good as I had not touched the collection money. I was only deluding myself anyway, as the collection money was locked up anyway. To even think about taking the collection money reveals where my mind was, I am afraid to say. She seemed sad when I left by taxi, and we did not kiss farewell. She waved to me, a forlorn, sad wave, half hiding behind the column by the door.

On the way to the airport, I had a Copt taxi driver. I asked him about Axum and if he had seen the carved churches in the rock…and I told him I wanted to visit the place. He seemed pleased that I asked him about where he was from and excitedly told me about his family and his Church's congregation here in Halifax. He wanted to talk about his new life in Canada, the future, not the troubles he had escaped from. And I just kept asking him about Axum. Back then, I didn't really understand all my travels had been imaginative; did I not know Kubla Khan's Xanadu was a vision in a dream?

***

I was returning to Toronto. Not Ottawa. That place was so full of shadows, falsehoods, scheming, plans of empty men. Memories that I knew would be awakened with new clamouring of mindless voices, parroting the cries of the latest trend. No, it would be Toronto. At least Toronto would buzz with the unheard voices of all the poor, the new, the hopeful Canadians, as well as the neglected old, with their walkers, fading memories and empty purses.

191

I had dressed nicely, and the check-in girl at the airport gave me a pass to the lounge. I think it is always important to dress nicely. I was pleased getting into the business lounge. I got a drink at the bar, and almost as soon as I got the drink, what seemed to me to be the archetypal international salesman with middle age spread sided up to me. He had an evening stubble, wore an azure blue suit, hailed from Bursa in Turkey, was proud to be a Kurd, and declared himself loudly to be a de facto supporter of Erdogan, "there is no other choice." I could see that a young Ottawa-CBC-leftie type seated at the next table was scowling, so I deliberately tried to draw him into the conversation. Unfortunately, he was one of those young ones today who knows all the answers – and assumes everyone agrees with him, as he is the one in possession of the "Truth" – but does not want anyone to question him and would never actually try to cogently defend his own views. He was the type to always express the flavour of the week – whether it be posting a Ukrainian flag on his Facebook this week, an "I hate Trump" meme last week, or an "I don't eat beef" sticker next week. One gets the impression that, despite his education, he never learned to think for himself. At least the Turk beside him could express and defend his views.

On the plane, I sat next to a bearded young man with a round face engulfed constantly by the loveliest smile. He talked not of money, ambition, success, and hard work but of kindness, his two children, his love for his wife, his religion, balance, nature, and – wait for it – cats. (But a man like this would like cats, wouldn't he?) Everything was great until I opened my handbag.

In it, I found an envelope from Beatrix. There was a note in the handbag, saying "Good luck, Helen," and five one-hundred-dollar bills. It was Les Misérables again, and I was Jean Valjean, offered silver candlesticks instead of a prison sentence.

Death, 145 BC

With Alexandria and the town of Balkh now burned, my manufactured daydreams only got worse. Nightmares over the death of Thaïs. The Saka had captured Thaïs and me. She was flayed alive: the flaying starting with the legs and moving upwards and inwards. This is the more painful death, rather than the quicker version that starts at the shoulders. Antiochus, captured earlier hiding in the temple of Juno, was given the old Persian torture of scaphism. It takes about two weeks to die. Tied between two small boats, his head, legs, and arms were extended beyond the boats. Continually force-fed honey and milk until he had to vomit; his limbs were then covered with the resultant puke, milk, and honey. Diarrhea eventually results. He could not move while bees, wasps, ants, beetles, and later, worms crawled in and all of his orifices. What they do to your eyes is the worst. They like the eyes especially; the moisture attracts them. It is the first part of the torture to cause the sufferer to scream. After trying to keep your eyelids shut, eventually, the eyelids' muscles relax in exhaustion, allowing the insects to feast. At first, they say, you can see and feel the insects on your eyes before you lose your sight.

I am lucky in the dream; they say that the Saka Khan felt sorry for me and gave me a broken glass in wine to drink. Luckily, I know the trick, having seen it used before. The idea is to drink as many pieces of broken glass as quickly as possible. The more cuts and rips in your digestive tract, the sooner you bleed to death through your anus and urethra. Drinking slowly and spitting out the big pieces of broken glass only means that you cut your tongue and mouth more, live longer, suffer more, and die even more painfully.

Yes, the Saka were so much more civilized than we were. Their promised world of peaceful co-existence was as fleeting as Antiochus' defence of the city had been before them.

***

Whether I was getting old, and my imagination was waning, or I just was giving up myself, I really stopped having these dreams and imagined worlds. I guess it couldn't get much worse once I was dead, anyway! But it is interesting how my earlier dreams when I was younger were of cities, vast, wide landscapes of mountains and valleys, and, when I got older, were of nearby scenes, immediate, short – and black in mood.

The Pilgrim's Progress, 2006

Now, Dante was in the middle of his life in the middle of a dark wood when he had his epiphany; mine was a little more prosaic, and it took some time for me to grasp what was happening. And I had a few setbacks. I was past the middle of my life, and Bloor St., unlike a forest, was well-lit. And I was alone as I had left Beatrix behind in Halifax – and I had no Vergil with me.

As we approached the island airport and banked and turned to land, the tall buildings seemed to rise out of the lake. To the east of them appears to be a small industrial wasteland of ruined buildings and abandoned factories, a contrast to the solid mass of concrete and steel high-rises that loom, Babel-like, stabbing the sky in their brash confidence. It is an impressive display of solidity, wealth, and raw power. It is a sweeping vista. We landed, and somehow, they had lost my luggage. Oh well.

Toronto has grand buildings. Walking between them and in the tunnels under the buildings, you feel small and insignificant. You really think of yourself as small. The tall windows look out over the highway towards the lake, and what a fabulous view it is. It was still early – the middle of the day – and I thought I would head for Bloor St.

But first, I stopped for a coffee at a little stand on the quay. The table I sat at had a wet stain of tea from a previous guest and a roll of cold cigarette ash, surrounded by a few soft flakes of random ash. Behind me drifted voices, male and female, mingling with a strong tobacco smell from cigarettes. I tried to listen, but I couldn't hear clearly, and it was more pleasing to think about how I had given up cigarettes and opioids. Cigarettes had been hard to give up. I still craved them – the smell of them is intoxicating to an ex-addict. Was this my only achievement to date? I looked out across Queens Quay West to one of those 24-hour variety stores and watched an older, stooping lady rocking uncertainly with every step she took toward the grocery shop. She seemed to be the type of mother to have given her entire life to her family. From across the street, the bright sun caught the magnificently deep blue and red patterns of her shawl that covered her hair and head. Perhaps she was from Trabzon, ancient Trebizond, from a religious and conservative family, from the Chepni Turkic tribe, who were themselves descendants of the Pechenegs who had fought and lost to the Byzantines all those centuries ago? And probably she knew nothing older of her family's history than watching her grandmother, toothless, helping her mother prepare dinner, talking of one day emigrating to Canada…

Just then, I heard that clicking of well-oiled pawls and hub teeth from a coasting bicycle, and I turned to see two young male cyclists in tight lycra going by. They could have been from the trendiest Toronto cycling club. They were young, successful, pleased with themselves, out enjoying the weather, and why not? Enjoy your salad days!

"Yes, we're taking a package tour to Bodrum," said a female voice behind. Bodrum! That is Halicarnassus! Turkey's Riviera! Where King Mausolus was buried by his sister-wife Artemisia in one of the wonders of the ancient world…I was all ears now. I turned in my seat to get a better look. They were clearly lawyers as they talked of cases and judges. The trip to a resort on the Mediterranean would be her first with her new boyfriend, I gleaned. The woman speaking now was very different than the older lady shopping across the street – this one was young, petite, pretty, trying to make sure whoever she was talking to knew she was going places and that her practice was successful. Well, Herodotus tells us how Artemisia fought bravely with Xerxes against the Greeks at the Battle of Salamis (Xerxes says of her fighting – she recovered his brother's body as well – "my men have become women; and my women, men") and certainly this young lawyer exhibited leadership, too. I could well believe she was going places. At one time, I was going places myself… Well, it has been a long time since the Luwians, the Greeks, the Persians, the Carians, the Crusaders, and now the Turks started visiting Halicarnassus. And now this pretty lawyer was going there, too? And what memories now remained of all these endeavours? All the money and culture of King Mausolus had not helped him. How brief, unimportant, and uneventful are our lives…as we all must eventually come to acknowledge.

I walked up Yonge St. Yonge St., if it ever were memorable, it is now nothing but totally forgettable – it is certainly not Chicago's

Magnificent Mile. What makes a great city? Walking up Michigan, past the Wrigley building, across the bridge, lights reflected, twinkling, in the river; lips chapped from the wind off the lake; the Windy City indeed. Past shops of lovely clothes, food, wines, and toys with pretty women walking past...all the things to please a woman's heart. I can see myself dancing the night away, music and stories, and memories of camaraderie. Surely, it is only 100 years from the Prohibition; drinks at the Coq d'Or at the Drake...the imagination starts to swim.

But Toronto is no Chicago. They say Shanghai is arriving – but Chicago has already arrived. There is a sense of fading grandeur as the New World becomes the Old World and as China rises. But did someone forget Toronto along the way? Will Toronto ever have such faded grandeur? Any memories of grand hotels? Will Toronto have its Al Capone, snake oil salesmen pedalling fake medicines, a Charles Dickens fighting for his royalties from pirated books?

Toronto has enough restaurants. An enormous pork chop – how big was the pig it came off – sat lonely in the window I passed. The glass caught the reflection of the wind blowing a pretty girl's shoulder-length hair, and as I turned to catch a glimpse of her, I caught her rich, pungent perfume that reached up your nostrils...and gently receded into a comfortable soft smell. It is strange that as I have grown older, I love perfume more and more....deep, rich, sophisticated...

Traffic was building as I reached Bloor St. Shoppers were everywhere; everyone seemed to have radiant smiles. And where had that pretty girl who had walked into my life and then, right out of it, gone? Her perfume had been overwhelming. She was radiant smiling, and her eyes sparkled with pleasure as she looked in the shop windows. Perfume was her last weapon; there she was! Passing the doorman, you could see he was clearly taken by her appearance – and perhaps by that strong, almost sharp, waves of perfume that still reached up deep into my nostrils in one powerful sweep and then gently receded back into a comforting, dulled, ever-presence. Both of them seemed so unconditionally happy; it was uplifting and made me smile too. It was good to be alive. Maybe it was ephemeral, but sometimes even the ephemeral is divine.

She had walked into the Windsor Arms Hotel; it was now many years since I had last walked in through the revolving doors, past the doorman, to the small and narrow elevator. It reflected an age that has gone. The small aperitif bar beside the elevator had dark wood panelling over the walls, and the low ceiling was dark with wooden beams. Years and coats of paint had masked the finer delineation of wood grain. It was the kind of ambience I liked; small, distinctive, and unique; modest yet nicely appointed.

I followed her. I was now walking in the steps I had taken so many years ago, as a young girl, with so much promise ahead. Back then, I remember the cold night air of the door closing behind me as I walked out. That chapter has ended. The door was a timekeeper for me, and I would not forget it. And here I was again, returning. What nostalgia! No, it was more than thirty years apart. I walked in, tall, slim, erect, and confident, across their threshold. Looking in the mirror as I passed, I noticed the wrinkles in the corner of my eyes, but that was a small price to pay. I was inwardly pleased. I had not, as my mother had warned me, "let myself go." I looked respectable, mature, and yet presentable and unpretentious. I looked nice in the white, fitted blouse and black pencil skirt. I sat in the bar, surely in the same chair I had sat in long ago. It was in the corner; it had a good view of both the bar and of the outside, with windows looking out on Sultan St. and to St. Thomas St. I ordered a drink. Time passed. My imagination started to run rampant…

Max was his name. He was tall and had broad shoulders, a smile that started small and grew across his face. And as it grew, he turned his head a little onto the side. Whereas all those years ago, the men had been much older than me, Max was younger, much younger. He came up to me in the bar and asked me if I was waiting for anyone.

"I was waiting for you," I replied. That little smile started, the tiniest admission of amusement, and then it slowly grew across his face from ear to ear, followed by a funny laugh. He was funny. I asked if I could buy him a drink.

"I do want a drink, but I insist on paying for yours, too." He was very attractive. And he was very attentive. He was in the advertising business. He could laugh at himself. We talked until the sky began to darken. We had some food. Then he looked me all over and said, "Since you are all dressed up to go out, let's go to El Mocambo."

"I like dancing," I said.

"I do too, though I usually only stay long enough for two drinks and two girls in the washroom before I leave."

"Max, you'll find one is enough tonight. And I don't do bathrooms." He had a Porsche; I loved it. We went dancing, and then we went back to his house in Rosedale. The moon had risen. At least, I thought it was his house.

"It's been more than twenty years since I was last on Roxborough," I said, reducing the number of years to pretend I was younger than I was.

"And twenty years since you were last with a man?"

"Not quite, Max."

We made love. We talked. Normally, I don't talk much. I did tonight. We went to the kitchen to eat something – I hadn't eaten much, and his mother came down to chat.

"It is a lovely house you have," I ventured. His mother smiled and seemed totally at ease with an older woman being in her kitchen at 3:00 a.m. with her son. She took a bowl of Jell-O out of the fridge. She may even have been younger than me. Later, she even gave me a toothbrush. She seemed quite amused that I had just arrived from Halifax without my bag, already knew Toronto, and yet had arrived with no place to stay. Max had offered me a taxi, but I really needed a place to crash – and luckily, his mother could see my exhaustion. She offered me a spare bedroom and let me sleep until late. It was a nice gesture, as the flying, the walking, the dancing, and my amatory activities were tiring. Sadly, I am no longer a spring chicken. Max was young and a tad too eager – though I did try to teach him how to kiss. I thought Max's mother was nice. But perhaps a little too indulgent to her son.

By the time I got up, Max had gone to work, and the mother and I had breakfast together. I didn't ask her if they knew the Emersons down the street. I really wanted to know but could not bring myself to ask. I told her I was now off to visit Taliska's and Adur's restaurant, "It's called 'La Churrascada.' I hear it has the best food! I knew them when I was at Vic." I now planned to show up, more than thirty years after last seeing them, unannounced.

"Oh yes, I've been there. It is very good."

I never even asked her name. As I left, she waved to me, "Come again!" I couldn't but think I could have been her, living on Roxborough, waving to the girlfriend of my son, had I done the normal thing and married Paul…

It had been at that breakfast, while the mother cooked me eggs Benedict, that I realized I had had an epiphany. Taliska and Adur should have been, and yet could still be, the centre that would hold.

Taliksa and Adur were what I was missing. Or they represented what I was missing. The centre that would not hold had been my life until now.

La Churrascada (The Barbecue), 2006

"Oh, I'd like to see Taliska and Adur when they have a moment," I said to the maître d', who looked quite young and quite flustered. The restaurant was very busy and clearly getting ready for a big function – and people were already arriving.

"Oh, I am sorry we are closed for a wedding," he replied. He had a name tag, 'Lorenzo,' on his chest. "Oh, that is O.K., Lorenzo; I am a great waitress, and I am dressed for it, too! Don't worry. I went to school with Taliska, and I know an extra pair of hands always comes in handy!"

"HELEN! HELEN! My God! Adur, Helen is here! Adur, come quick!" Taliska rushed towards me with tears flowing, arms outstretched, crying loudly, all smiles and eagerness! All those years gone by, and what a welcome!

***

It was a lovely wedding! The virtue of ritual and tradition. The families joining were first-generation Canadians, originally from the small town of Barad in Syria, just 20 miles or so from Aleppo. Barad is one of the 700 dead – mostly Christian – cities of Syria; abandoned settlements from pre-Hittite, Hittite, Old Babylonian, Old Assyrian, Aramean, New Assyrian, Achaemenid, Greek, Roman, Byzantine, Sassanid, Umayyad, Byzantine again under Nikephoros II Phokas, Seljuqs and Ayyubids, Mongols and

Mamluks, Ottoman times....war has crisscrossed the Levant for thousands of years. Today, if anything, it is worse as America cements its hegemony by fomenting proxy wars here and yet does not kill its own soldiers but uses those of other countries to die for it, selling its weapons in the process. America sits back and smiles as more innocents die as it puts more of its puppets on thrones. It is all for freedom and liberty, you know.

These two families, everyday-average Sunnis, rejoicing in the wedding of their son and daughter, care not for the suffering of Syria over the centuries but only for their living family members. They do not need more worries – but thanks to America, they do.

After hugging Taliska and Adur, I was busy around the tables, bringing water and serving the celebratory yerba maté drink. They did not drink the alcoholic arak, the Levantine anise. I was told that Barad is a small agricultural town known for its apricots, figs, and grapes. It is hard not to enjoy a wedding; the bride and groom's families are happy to share their best wishes with the world. The collegiality of a small town, the richness of its heritage, and the combined efforts of all to share happiness are contagious.

A sudden downpour appeared, requiring the wedding to move indoors, just before the groom was carried in. The move was impressively achieved, and soon the bride and groom entered and the party began in earnest! Barad is clearly NOT a town for the jet-setters, and custom has it that much of the entertainment of the wedding is watching the performance of its actors. They had not forgotten their roots. Of course, not knowing Levantine Arabic, I missed the significance of the vows and rituals. I thoroughly enjoyed the dancing, the music, and the obvious happiness. You smiled when you saw the young men's and the young women's eyes meet and you sensed their excitement when they danced. It was refreshing and made you feel good. This is what our brief lives are about: courting and eventual procreation. Theirs is not a culture of relaxed sexual mores. I particularly enjoyed the traditional "country" dancing, which seems universal around the world with its constricting and expanding circles, joined arms alternatively rising and falling, legs moving in time to the music, with smiles all around. It is good to be alive and good to just watch. (Although one curmudgeon beside me, who said he was a retired army officer, complained to me about the use of electronics and the addition of the "Saudi beat" to traditional Syriac musical instruments!)

I met the family, countless relatives, luminaries, retired and respected folk, and many children. The children were adorably shy. It is to our shame that North Americans denigrate shyness, modesty, and humility. I once read somewhere that the American Psychiatric Association considers shyness a defect, like autism. God knows we have much to be modest about, starting with our narcissism. I should know. The elders here, like people everywhere, just want a simple life, happiness for their children – and peace. Weddings are, of course, a microcosm of what is possible when goodwill abounds. It is too bad they are so fleeting.

After another scene of adorably innocent children being children, I asked Lorenzo beside me if Taliska and Adur had any children. He looked at me sideways, startled, and said, "They had a daughter. She and her husband were burned – churrasco! – in a car accident". He snapped his fingers as he said 'churrasco,' as if to say 'gone, just like that.' He continued, "Their daughter, Emily, survived."

I must have looked horrified, so he continued, "Yes, two Haitians stole a BMW X5, ran a red light, hit their little Kia, rolled it over, and it caught fire. Somehow, people rescued Emily in the back."

By the time the cleaning and washing up was done, it was late. Adur was still scrubbing pans, and I was drying glasses when Taliska approached me, saying, "Thank you for your help today; it was a big help. Can you stay with us tonight? You can meet our granddaughter tomorrow morning – Little Emily".

"I'd love to. You are always so kind".

The next day was Sunday, and the restaurant was closed. I told my stories; she told me her recent news. The car accident was recent; within the last year, and the wound was still fresh. Apparently, the car theft was not even to ship the car to the Middle East, or something. It was stolen just for a lark by two Haitians illegally in Canada. Taliska and Adur did not want to talk about it. It had been a glancing hit, killing her daughter instantly, and the husband had been pinned between the 'A' column and the steering wheel, dying slowly and painfully. Overturned by the BMW, the car slid on the asphalt, which sparked the metal and ignited spilled gasoline. History repeats itself with another Françoise Dorléac killed in an overturned burning car. An old man walking past had been able to get Emily out of the car seat in the back.

Emily herself was a dear, alert, bright, and an early talker.

"Helen, I have Christiaan's address here," Taliska said, matter-of-factly.

The Joy of Loyalty, 2006 - 2007

I sent an email to Christiaan, asking if I could pop by the next day. He replied instantly. The world does not stand still. That night, through the open window of Taliska's spare bedroom, still decorated with her daughter's childhood heartthrobs, teddy bears, and stuffed pussycats, I heard an owl hooting at me. I left after breakfast.

Christiaan lived in what I call a Toronto 'strawberry-box' house. Small, compact with steep roofs and three bedrooms, they dot East York. Called Victory Housing, they had been built for returning veterans after WWII. I felt like a returning veteran – although not one that had won a war – walking up to the door.

He greeted me with a small smile when he opened the door. "It's been a long time; come in, andante con moto."

"Thank you," I said, giving him a little kiss on the cheek as I entered. He didn't expect it; he had a warm cheek. He led me to the sitting home on the left as you enter. "I love these houses - I think they were built on a 17th century New England plan – there were a whole bunch of them by Westgate Shopping Centre in Ottawa – I love them – do you remember them, behind the Lucky Key Restaurant?"

"Yes, I do – the restaurant that was caught twice cooking the neighbours' cats, not once, but twice?" We smiled together at the shared memory, and he continued, "I like my little house. You must see my garden…"

"Thank you for inviting me here, Christiaan," I interrupted.

"Helen, our years are short, and our doom is that the flame burns quickly…" He clearly wanted to take me to his garden, as he was trying to shepherd me to the back door…

"Christiaan, tell me what happened."

"Oh, you are funny, Helen. After all these years of ignoring me, we meet for one minute, and you are pressing the button to 'Go'! You should never have jumped to conclusions. The clock was high up and heavy. I went up, got it, brought it down, fixed it. Nothing to it. Just dust and oil making a sludge. Those clocks are indestructible; wipe the sludge out and they keep good time. The clock was installed far too high on the wall. I put it back up on the wall. He didn't like how I had put it and wanted it straightened his way. I told him not to go up the ladder and that I would do it, but he would not listen. He went up the ladder, the clock was heavy, and then he fell off the ladder. At least, that is how it always looked to me."

"But they say nothing about him falling off a ladder at the time. Are you sure he fell...?"

"No, the doctor said it was nothing about falling off the ladder. The doctor said it was a brain bleed and that he fell AFTER the bleed, a subarachnoid haemorrhage. They could tell from where his bleed was and where his head hit the ground…"

"No!"

"I thought you knew. I never thought you did NOT know. An haemorrhagic stroke. The autopsy determined where the bleeding was, and it didn't correlate with the injury of the fall. You know, how far the fall was, and how hard he hit the floor, right? It was a long time ago."

"No, I didn't know. I thought you pushed him," I said quietly. "As I asked you. I asked you to kill him, and then you did what I asked. You would do what I asked; I knew it then, and I know it now."

"Ahhh. But I knew you were upset and did not really mean it." A silence descended upon the room. "Let's go and look at my trees…" We walked into the back garden. Although the back garden was quite small, there were two adolescent trees, already climbing high, a walnut and a ginkgo.

"A society grows great when old men plant trees under which they will never sit," said Christiaan proudly as we looked up at them.

"They are already big enough to sit under," I replied.

"Yes, and now you are going to tell me what you have done all these years, Helen. You will have done things I have never dreamed of."

"I am not interested in remembering."

"But I want to live through your life's adventures."

"I live for now. The past is gone. I don't care about it. I want to live now, with you."

He had never married, had taken early retirement from an internal audit job with the provincial government, and split his time looking after his aged mother in Ottawa and gardening. I could tell he still looked at me wistfully, but his hair was white, he wore glasses, and he shuffled a bit. I told him a sanitized version of my troubles as humankind cannot suffer too much reality.

I tried to be useful and spent two days just cleaning his bathroom. His never marrying and living alone showed. I wanted to be useful and the place, well, it was filthy. I refused money from him. He had not been judgemental (even the diluted version of my story had caused his eyes to open wider and wider) and he had unhesitantly shared his small house with me – not an easy thing to do for someone accustomed to being on his own. I stayed out of his way, watching from a distance.

Hours he spent on his tomato patch produced this large tomato, which he proudly gave to me. He must have spent hundreds of hours on this plant, weeding around it, watering, propping up branches, encouraging it to grow – I think I even heard him coaxing the sun to come out. (I jest, but he was so earnest!) He was devastated with the results. The tomato, now ripe, was prepared for a salad. The skin was too thick; it peeled like the thick skin of a sow's ear; the seeds inside were huge and indigestible, and the watery inside was pale and tasteless. The more I complimented his efforts, the more upset he seemed to be. I told him the soil must have been sterile and the next day, he was out there inspecting it.

His mornings were spent in his garden and afternoons reading. In the evening, he watched television. Sundays, he went to Church. His life was regimented. He asked nothing of me, offering suggestions only to my questions. Nothing was too much; he was a trusting, kind, and good man. A lovely man. He was normal. Nothing extraordinary. A few peccadillos, a few odd habits, but hey, what did I care? An ordinary man, with an ordinary ambition, and expecting nothing extraordinary. I tried to interest him in me; at one point, I got an invitation, finally, from a successful acquaintance from school and dressed up for lunch downtown. I wore thigh-high stockings and provided Christiaan a suitably modest but interesting glimpse of harmless thigh. His eyes were interested, and maybe his mind, but I could not build upon it, sadly. I was still up for sex.

***

One day he returned from the doctors, and before he thanked me for cooking his favourite meat pie, which he always did, he told me he had pancreatic cancer. I was shocked. But then I noticed his jaundiced look; that first but painless indicator that the bile cannot clear the liver, that unmistakable sign something is amiss. He started to go downhill almost immediately. He was only two years older than me. His regimen changed quickly. He decided on palliative care; nausea and pain control were our operative objectives. He needed me more; almost every week, he was able to do less. Soon,

I was bathing and shaving him. Luckily, I was always a strong girl, and he was of a slight build. I liked looking after him. He was so gentle and asked so little. His legs mottled early.

"Helen, I am dying. To me, you were white apple blossoms. Everything passes. No, do not cry, do not regret! We are withering gold leaves. Do you remember talking about Lothlórien and the elves having to leave Middle Earth? I thought of you as Galadriel".

"Galadriel had her memories," I replied sadly.

"Yes."

"Dear Christiaan, you have had a useful life; you have played your part, you have not kicked away the gifts given you, as I have done. You stayed true to your ideals. You never faltered. Of course, we are insignificant in time and place when you think of the numberless and ageless stars. But we only bloom for a day, and you can stand fair and square on Judgement Day. You'll be fine."

As time passed, his pain seemed to increase, and I spent my days and nights beside his bed. I read and talked to him. He did have a pain pump, which he could control, but it did not seem to provide much relief. As his pain increased, he lost control of his bowels, and he was very embarrassed. Now I had to change sheets, do the laundry, and help him move in and out of the bed. And, of course, soiling himself and the bed does not happen when the visiting nurse came to visit for two hours twice a week – so I got more experience and practice than I wanted. Defecation is awful. It was at this point I sent a cheque to Beatrix, and this was hard to do. I included a note about my theft and my apology and repeated inconsiderateness. It seemed the right thing to do. I don't know if she replied, I never saw a reply. Overdue, at least I did the right thing.

That night, the rain fell hard and fast, pounding on the old tin garbage can by the garage. He lingered for what seemed a long time, more than a month at least, often drifting in and out of consciousness. It was a long and painful death for what seemed a blameless man.

At the end, I was with him when he died. He, who had been so opposed to my use of opioids and now so dependent upon them – yet he still tried to fight taking them. He was in pain and drugged, but he grabbed my hand and said, "I don't want to die." I squeezed his hand and told him I loved him and that no one wants to die. Even though he was drifting in and out of delirium, he seemed to hear. His eyes, oh so gentle, looked at me, and he smiled, one last, short, simple smile that is forever burned in my memory.

After what seemed a long time of that awful Cheyne–Stokes periodic breathing, which bothers the listeners more than the sufferers, there was a long last gasp, a ghastly death rattle. Then he was gone. His eyes were wide open, and his face had frozen with fear. It was really upsetting.

The Necropolis, 2007

The Necropolis is a quiet and historical place. Our culture denies death's inevitable calling. We don't talk about death. But it is coming, nonetheless. The Toronto Necropolis is that place that shows its victory over human vanity, greed, and emptiness. It has always held a special place for me, overlooking the Don River, filled with history and forgotten stories of lives lived. How many sad lives, how many happy lives, have been stilled and buried here? Who remembers them now? Is everything futile if it is to be forgotten? What does the Necropolis do except remind us of what we have lost and are about to lose?

I buried Christiaan where he wanted to be buried. I was able to get him a lovely spot on the headland. I think it was my faded beauty and the story I told of how long I had known Christiaan, that got me such a good plot from the quiet and respectful salesgirl, Tara Pryke. You could see how she cared, and it was lovely. Once again, I was a Taker, getting that valuable, reserved spot. I walked to the edge and looked down to Bayview Ave, choked with stationary – idling – cars in four lanes, as this was before the two empty bicycle lanes. Further out, I could see the slow, polluted Don River and the rusting, amputated, Old Eastern Ave truss bridge, going from nowhere to nowhere. Now dead and unnoticed, that single abandoned span had once been the route out to the West....

Irony. Life is about irony, the recognition of the incongruities of life. Yes, our lives have differing meanings and perspectives, depending upon the angles from which we look and the effects that the illusions we create in our and others' minds are powerful, but it all depends upon irony – all is not what it seems to be at first glance or expectation. There is more. We usually see it long after what has happened; this gives us empathy and a richer appreciation of life. Much of the meaning of our lives come from these waves of empathy over the years as we suffer setbacks and achieve what we think are successes. It is a gift seldom appreciated. Indeed, Arion was saved from drowning as he was carried to the shore by the dolphins who loved his music and his voice…

Snowflakes were swirling in the cold air. They played and danced on their way down, with not a care in the world for you or for me. It was a bitter December, a harbinger of the worst January to come. Having no gloves, I buried my hands deep into my pockets. Christiaan had been real for me, unchanging, steadfast, and constant all the years of his life. Standing there in the cold, with him gone, I suddenly felt as though I knew him and now finally knew what I had lost. Loyalty.

I have chased and fled from dreams across this vast land of ours, and while it is nothing compared with the expanse of our universe, with untold billions of stars and unknowns, it is my own little life. While my journey has been as insignificant as my accomplishments, I do know that when mine ends, others begin and continue. But what Christiaan taught me was to understand that there is a blissful leap into eternity – faced with fear and trembling, of course – but available – for all of us. There is more to life than ourselves. And you don't learn this only from books. It has to be lived. It was that recognition I had to make myself to escape that last enemy, which is not only death itself but me. I turned back towards the glorious lychgate at the Necropolis and its companion chapel, nestled under comforting trees.

I think it was Friedrich von Schiller who wrote of 'liebesschmerz' – one of those great compound words that Germany has given the world – 'love-pain'; those feelings that even if love passes, the pain remains of what has been lost. As I was walking back from his grave, though, I thought now not of Christiaan but rather of a time with Boaz. I haven't mentioned it to you. He had been invited to a gala ball at the Westin Vancouver by 'the Catholic Club' – but what the 'Catholic Club' was, he could not, or would not, tell me. I was pleased he was taking me and not his wife. It was a big deal, and there were people coming from all over the world. From the use of code words he had used in other conversations, I knew he was getting some revolvers and handguns for some of the bodyguards of the attendees. I doubt it had anything to do with any Catholic Clubs I thought of when I thought of the Roman Catholic Church's services for its parishioners.

He picked me up in his Jaguar V12 (I think I also forgot to mention it was one of the rare and fancy V12s) from my apartment, and we drove to the Westin. He had a suite with a balcony overlooking Vancouver Harbour, Stanley Park, and towards Capilano. It was as nice as it gets. On the bed was a box. In the box was the most beautiful, short, off-the-shoulder, organza silk black dress layered with tulle. Naturally, the tulle was silk. The dressmaker's address was Bellagio, Lake Como. Wow. Lake Como! For me, it was a place of dreams filled with rich and accomplished people and the best of everything. It fit perfectly. How was he able to get that made for me in Italy? More importantly, how was the dressmaker able to show off my tits the way he did? There is not much support available without straps – remember, I have big, full ones and need some support – yet I looked more than fantastic. And this was done without a fitting?

There were speeches, some 200 people (many were, it seemed, bodyguards), and Boaz got an award for something. They didn't really explain what it was for, and Boaz certainly wasn't about to tell me. I was seated next to an older American officer with lots of gold braids and what seemed to be a large burn scar covering much of his face. He talked intensely to Boaz before he sat down.

I asked him to dance with me, and, being the consummate gentleman, he obliged. I am not a great ballroom dancer, and he was an excellent lead. I think many women underestimate the pleasure of being led on the dance floor to beautiful music while men watch them. I guess it helps to be pretty. I will never forget the dance, an excellent performance of Shostakovich's Waltz #2 – I did say this was a fancy do – and he was a lovely dancer. Surely only someone who lived under Stalin could have written such a haunting melody! Uneasy, edgy, moving from light to dark, it opens with a march-like sequence, before that haunting melody is heard, played by the saxophone, before being passed around the orchestra. By turns blithe, merry, and gay, deeply wistful, then yearning and nostalgic: for a moment, splendid, almost triumphant; only to become menacing, bitter, and deeply tragic. Ah! That melody played against the unrelenting, ominous bass line played on the double basses and snare drum; what memories! What a fool I had been all those years ago! He said his name was Colonel Farnsworth – I assume he was telling me his real name and his nametag said that. I did try my usual charms with him, smiles, standing close yet remaining gentle the normal coy stuff – and it seemed to be working. So, I thought I could ask him about Boaz.

"Did you get that scar on operations with Boaz?" I asked him.

"He warned me about you, Helen," he replied. I wish we could have danced all night.

The Colonel was accompanied by a younger man, a more junior officer, who sat on his other side.

"Is your friend, Chad, beside you, your spouse?"

"No, he is my First Sergeant."

"Oh, he is your batman, your valet?"

"We don't have batmen in the Marines."

"Then he is your bodyguard?"

"Boaz tells me you are a great violin player, Helen."

As you can tell, I didn't learn much from him.

That night, in the bedroom, after great sex – Boaz bent me over the chair while I was still in the dress – ripping off the pantyhose –

we stood on the balcony and looked at the moon and its long, straight shadow across the bay. It was peaceful. It was lovely.

Then he said, "I don't want you to be another Lakshmi." Lakshmi, the previous girlfriend, reared her head again. "She died saving my life," he continued. His eyes had that far-away look where nothing present here and now exists. He looked out over the bay. You can imagine my thoughts.

He wouldn't tell me more about Lakshmi. Lakshmi. Where did she come from? How did they meet? What happened to her, and when? I was jealous of Lakshmi and wanted that spot in his heart she had. And she had saved his life…she was obviously useful to him, unlike me. He just said, with a gentle smile, "Helen, you think no one could have a past before you came along."

But it was only now that it all dawned on me. I'm a late developer, you might say. It wasn't about sex. It was about love. Lakshmi and Boaz had something special, something so far beyond what I could over-analyze in my complex brain. Boaz was driven. He believed in something. He had ideals. He was not able to be moved from what he had to do. I may not understand what it was, but he was on a mission. He had a duty to do something, and he was going to do his duty. Boaz's stature rose even larger in my eyes. Lakshmi loved him and intuitively saw what I had not seen: his mission and his duty. Loving him dearly, she did for him what she could do when she had to do it. That's the difference.

The wind had picked up, and it was now bitterly cold. With the taste of salty, running tears in my mouth, I walked past the markers of others' lives of love and thought tenderly of Lakshmi:

A Gift

Was it a bullet that came for him
That you, stepping forward,
Bravely, took?

That swept you away
Lying at his feet,
Broken, dead?

Cruel, Cruel
A part of him died
That day.

Lying at his feet.
A silent, glazed gaze:
An unholy sacrifice.

*

Know he walks with you still,
Holding your hand,
With the same pace and step.

But of course, dear Lakshmi
You know this already,
And always knew this.

He will always be by your side
Looking for your hand.
He loves you, and only you.

The gift you gave
He wishes you had kept

Still reaching for your hand.

*

Oh Lakshmi
He still reaches for your hand,
Searching for you.

And now that I had buried honest Christiaan, I was thinking of Boaz.

Again.

***

Another Copt taxi driver drove me back to the empty house. Growing up, I had never met a Copt or even known what a Copt was. When I got home, all was dark with the lights off in that unwelcoming, late autumn feel of cold, short days filled with loneliness and emptiness. I was depressed and back in the Slough of Despond. I had found Christiaan, and he had taken me in. And, unlike the Hired Man, he did NOT have to take me in. It was lonely to lose him. He was a lovely man, even though I had spent most of my time thinking of Boaz and Lakshmi in the cemetery. Between the screen door and front door was a brown envelope from 'Simmons and Meyer, Barristers and Solicitors,' stamped as 'confidential', no less.

Going inside, I turned on the lights, saw that there was a flashing light on my ancient answering machine, and opened the envelope. Inside was a letter and a long legal document. On the cover letter was a handwritten note:

"Helen, I was really pleased to find you as the beneficiary of Christiaan de Klerk's will. He set up this will and appointed me Executor some ten years ago before his parents died in Ottawa. Upon his recent death, his file was transferred to me here at our Toronto office, and I have attached a copy of it for your records. We've already set up the ownership transfer of the house and of his bank accounts, survivor pension, investments, etc., to be transferred to you upon your approval, signatures, and instructions.

Helen, I have never forgotten how you trounced me in that Moot Case all those years ago. We all sat mesmerized by your speech! You carried the day with your arguments! I've been carrying a torch for you all these years, and if you are up for it, I'd love to grab lunch with you – or just a coffee if time is pressing.

Regards, **Gerhard**."

Who the hell is Gerhard? I thought. I don't remember any Gerhard. I looked at the attachments. Gerhard Meyer: Now, there is a German pining for me after all these years? And the irony of ironies, the lies of my Moot addresses to the jury that day were not only good enough to be believed at that time, but to be remembered all these years later? And this Gerhard has no idea that my tongue was in my cheek, that I believed the opposite of what I said? Or maybe he did – and that is why he likes me? All I could think of was

Marlene Dietrich's "Du, du, liegst mir am Herzen...you, you, are close to my heart." As though all I needed now was another lovesick victim!

Well, this was all a surprise. Christiaan had never said anything about any will...A rather nice surprise, though, come to think of it. I was wondering where – and how – I was going to live.

I did painfully note, however, that I had never even asked Christiaan about how his parents were doing back in Ottawa on Avondale Ave...or did they live on Tweedsmuir? There is no fairness in this world. I continued to be offered more than I deserved.

I went to pick up the messages, expecting an offer for duct cleaning services from Mumbai but decided to ignore it when I saw a 604-area code – Vancouver. Why did I want to talk to a voice from my past?

Christmas, 2007

From the distance, the gentle breeze made the Christmas lights look as though they were blinking when really it was only the branches gently swaying. It wasn't cold today. It was just that wet snow temperature, which is not so bad. It was Christmas, and so I was in a good mood anyway. I love Christmas. I approached the happy house. When Adur opened the door, the refrain "Noël, Noël, chantons le Rédempteur!" of 'O Holy Night' was belting out loud and clear, and little Emily came bounding to the door, crying "Hi Auntie Helen!" What a hymn! What a welcome! What a night it was to be! Indeed, as I look back on that night, I am still on my knees, trembling with gratitude and hope.

It was perfect; the conversation, the food, the songs, the drinks, the Christmas crackers, everything was the best it could be, and I was unfairly blessed yet again.

"Auntie Helen, what should I be when I grow up?"

"What do you like to do, Emily?"

"I can't decide between being a pilot or a doctor."

"Well, they are both great professions. You don't have to make up your mind today. There is lots of time. And you may like something different five years from now."

"How will I know, Auntie?"

"Well, you have sensible grandparents – Grandma Taliska and Granddad Adur. You should watch them, listen to them, do what they suggest, learn from them, and, above all, always do your best. They will be your best guides in life. They love you, and they want the best for you. They will always be rooting for you. Only do what they would do; if you don't know, ask them. They want to help. Listen to them. That way, you will always know what you should do."

***

Now, when most people were thinking of retiring, I had finally found my calling. Taliska and Adur wanted me in their lives, and little Emily (for some strange reason!) adored me. Emily was a bright girl and enraptured as I began to teach her music, science, and the humanities. If I could, I would repay Adur's and Taliska's kindness, loyalty, and belief in me after all the years the locusts had eaten.

Despite my years of just taking rather than giving, there were others out there who did believe in the goodness of others – and, even more, amazing to me, there were people out there who knew me and still believed in me despite my dismal record! And, you know what, with money from Christiaan, maybe I could make a difference to help others who were less fortunate. What a reversal in my life had come about. The fact is that I had enjoyed helping (in my small and insignificant way) both Joelle and Christiaan. I had a purpose, and now a mandate, to try and think of others. And who knew what tomorrow might bring?

The dolphins had returned to rescue me one more time.

Manufactured by Amazon.ca
Acheson, AB

11960027R00131